BREATHING ROOM

ONE MAN'S PATH FROM PERFORMANCE TO PRESENCE

TEDD SIMMONS

ISBN: 979-8-89694-991-6 - Ebook
ISBN: 979-8-89694-992-3 - Paperback
ISBN: 979-8-89694-993-0 - Hardcover

To Tavo—

My partner on an adventure towards authenticity and in life. You have always believed in me and encouraged me to press forward, no matter the obstacles ahead. Your faith and unwavering support have been my strength, and your love has been my compass.

You are the man who made a difference.
You are the one who changed me forever.

This work is dedicated to you.

TABLE OF CONTENTS

PROLOGUE

THE WEIGHT OF SILENCE

There's a particular kind of exhaustion that comes from performing your life instead of living it. It settles in your bones like winter cold, persistent and penetrating, seeping through every carefully constructed layer until even your dreams feel rehearsed. For decades, I carried this weight the burden of being perfectly acceptable to everyone except myself.

I became a master of translation, converting my authentic thoughts into palatable versions, my genuine reactions into appropriate responses. I learned to speak in code, to love in whispers, to exist in the margins of my own story. The real me lived in the spaces between words, in the pause before I answered, "How are you?" in the careful edit of every emotion before it reached my face.

You know this performance, don't you? The way you've trained yourself to laugh at jokes that aren't funny, to nod along with conversations that make your soul recoil, to present a version of yourself that's been focus-grouped by fear and approved by other people's comfort levels. The way you've become so fluent in this second language of acceptability that sometimes you forget what your native tongue sounds like.

This exhaustion isn't dramatic. It doesn't arrive with fanfare or crisis. It accumulates like dust, like interest on a debt you never agreed to take on. It's in the slight delay before you respond to your own name, the way you catch yourself mid-gesture and course-correct, the hollow feeling that follows every successful performance of who you're supposed to be.

This is the story of how I learned to breathe again, not the shallow, careful breathing of someone afraid to take up too much space, but the deep, unconscious breathing of someone who belongs in their own life.

It's not about any single aspect of identity, though identity is woven throughout. It's a story about the courage required to be fully human in a world that prefers us in digestible pieces, sorted and labeled and stripped of the beautiful contradictions that make us whole.

It's about the price we pay for others' comfort, the slow erosion of self that happens when we consistently choose harmony over honesty, acceptance over authenticity. It's about the subtle violence of a thousand small compromises, each one seemingly insignificant, until one day you realize you can't remember the last time you said what you actually meant.

But more than that, it's about the revolution that happens when we finally refuse to pay this price. Not the dramatic kind of revolution with banners and speeches, but the quiet, persistent revolution of showing up as ourselves, day after day, in a world that taught us we needed permission to exist.

It's about learning that our wholeness was never negotiable, that the parts of us we've been taught to hide or soften or apologize for are often the very parts that hold our power. It's about discovering that the thing we feared most, being truly seen, is the same thing we've been desperately longing for all along.

If you've ever felt like a stranger in your own skin, if you've ever smiled through the ache of invisibility, if you've ever wondered who you might be if fear wasn't writing your story, this is for you.

If you've ever stood at your own crossroads, knowing that the familiar path leads nowhere you want to go but terrified of what lies down the untraveled road, this is for you.

If you've ever been told, in words or silence, in looks or laws, in love offered conditionally, that your truth is too much, too little, too complicated, too simple, too anything other than exactly what it is, this is for you.

This is the story of learning to trust the voice that whispers underneath the performance, the one that remembers who you were before the world taught you who you should be. It's about finding your way back to that original self, not despite the journey you've taken, but because of it.

It's about discovering that silence, while it may feel safe, is never truly silent at all. It echoes. It reverberates through every relationship, every opportunity, every moment of potential connection. And sometimes, the bravest thing we can do is let ourselves be heard—first by ourselves, then by the world.

The weight of silence nearly broke me. But in learning to set it down, I found something I hadn't expected: not just my voice, but my breath, my space, my right to exist exactly as I am.

This is how I learned to breathe. This is how I learned to live.

And this is how you can too.

CHAPTER 1

THE ART OF DISAPPEARING

It's been thousands of years since this world began to evolve — millions, if you count from the first spark of breathless dust and molten possibility. And yet, for all the stars we've mapped, for all the lands we've charted and names we've carved into time… there is still so much we don't know. About the universe. About each other. About ourselves.

We humans have always discovered slowly, almost reluctantly. One truth at a time. We learned to build fire. Then we learned to burn each other with it. We invented words, then we learned how to twist them into silence. We split atoms before we understood how deeply we could split hearts.

But I'm not here to write a thesis on civilization. I'm here to talk about something far more complex than any galaxy I've studied through a telescope or culture I've glimpsed through books. I'm here to talk about the most confounding, miraculous, terrifying thing I've ever had to understand:

Me.

You see, human beings are not just bones, blood, or names on office doors. We're emotional… We're perception… We're millions of thoughts ricocheting around the glass walls of our minds every single second. We are a contradiction and chaos and poetry, no matter how cleanly we try to label ourselves. And yet, somewhere along the way, we decided to simplify ourselves.

We began to categorize each other. Straight. Gay. Man. Woman. Masculine. Feminine. Success. Failure. We built boxes, painted them in socially acceptable colors, and told people to live there. We taught children how to shrink their true selves into spaces designed by someone else.

And I… I lived in one of those boxes for far too long. But not anymore.

We were born into a world already breathtaking in its design. Nature crafted it that way: rivers flowing without apology, trees stretching toward the sun without fear of judgment, clouds shifting shape without asking permission. Everything just… exists. Wild, free, unapologetically itself.

But somehow, humans forgot we were part of that same nature. We began building something else, not cities or houses, but expectations, silent rules, invisible boxes.

We stopped just being and started performing. Somewhere between childhood and now, we learned to measure ourselves by standards we didn't set: skin tone, weight, career, clothing, relationships, and accolades. We painted masks with approval and wore them like a second skin.

And quietly, painfully, so many of us are still performing. Maybe not in theaters or stages, but in everyday life in classrooms, at dinner tables, on social media. Some of us are pretending to be who they need us to be just to be loved. Others are shrinking parts of themselves to feel safe. We've grown used to editing our truths, muting our joys, hiding the cracks that make us real.

Maybe that's you.

Maybe you've felt the ache of not fitting in, being too much or not enough. Perhaps you've whispered questions to yourself in the dark, wondering if anyone else feels this way. Maybe you've looked at your reflection and thought, If only they knew who I really am…

If so, you're not alone.

This book wasn't written only for a label, flag, or community. It's for every soul that's ever felt boxed in by someone else's definition of "normal." This is for anyone wanting to step outside the script and live honestly. It's for those still hiding, still healing, still learning that it's okay to be fully, imperfectly, unapologetically themselves.

So, if you've ever longed to breathe without bracing yourself first, stay. This story might begin with me, but it belongs to all of us.

So let me start by removing the ribbon of mystery before we go any further:

I'm gay.

Not just gay. A proud gay man.

And this story, my story, isn't one of shame. It's one of becoming. It's one of peeling back all the quiet layers, the polite lies, the well-dressed performances, and saying, "Here. This is me. No edits. No apologies."

If you're still reading, thank you.

Welcome to my world.

Buckle in, because you're about to ride shotgun on a roller coaster built with lonely nights, ruptured expectations, accidental laughter, and the quiet, thunderous triumph of acceptance.

Now, I can already hear the skeptics: "But you live in the West. Don't gay people have rights there?"

Yes. On paper. In parades. In some policies. In the polished diversity statements of large corporations.

But there's a difference between legal permission and emotional inclusion. There's a canyon between being tolerated and being understood. Just because something is allowed doesn't mean it's embraced. Just because I can marry doesn't mean I won't be mocked in the grocery store line. Just because I can hold a flag doesn't mean I won't lose a job for not acting "straight enough."

People often dismiss our pain by pointing at the progress: "You already have your rights. What more do you want?" And to that I say, "We want to stop surviving. We want to start living."

Let me take you back. Not twenty years. Not even thirty.

Let me take you back a few centuries to the spirit of the Victorian era. A time when a woman's voice in the public sphere was an act of rebellion. A time when the feminist movement was only beginning to echo through the halls of history. Women wanted to be seen as equals, to vote, to work, to exist beyond the margins assigned to them simply.

And now, more than a hundred years later, women are still fighting. Still marching. Still bleeding.

Just like that, the LGBTQ+ journey has only begun. Yes, we've had milestones. Yes, we've won battles. But the war? The war is far from over because we're still judged. Still stereotyped. Still placed into neat boxes that don't fit the souls we carry.

You see, being gay isn't one-size-fits-all. We don't all dance in feather boas or wear bright pink. Some of us wear work boots. Some of us teach. Some of us are doctors, carpenters, soldiers, poets, and engineers. We love differently, live authentically, yet we're told we must fit a certain image to be accepted as who we are.

I never fit that image. My body didn't betray me, and my voice didn't give me away. I looked like what society would call a "straight man," and so the burden was heavier. People didn't believe me. Or worse, they believed me and decided I was "confused" or "trying to be trendy."

Let me say this as clearly as possible: I am not a trend. I am not a phase. I am not an idea for your comfort. I am a human being with a soul that knows who it is.

So, when people ask me what I'm still fighting for, I want to take them back to every moment I held my breath at a family gathering, every time I laughed along when someone used the word "sissy" like a punchline, every Sunday dinner where I passed as straight just to be loved.

It takes energy to pretend. It takes strength to smile through rejection. It takes everything not to collapse under the weight of invisibility.

This is why I write and share, not for applause but for understanding. Maybe if more people heard what it was like to walk through life on tiptoe, afraid to be fully seen, they'd stop asking what more we want and start asking what they can do.

This is my journey. This is my truth. And you're holding it in your hands.

The journey is long. The road is uneven. But I am no longer afraid to walk it.

So, let's begin.

EARLY LESSONS IN PERFORMANCE

I learned to disappear long before I understood what I was hiding from.

It started with small corrections. Third grade, walking to the pencil sharpener. My teacher's laugh cutting through the classroom chatter: "Why do you walk like that?" The question landed like a stone in still water, sending ripples of silence across the room. I didn't know what she meant, but I understood the tone. Something about me was wrong.

That night, I practiced walking in my bedroom mirror. Shoulders back, hips still, each step deliberate and unremarkable. I was eight years old, learning my first lesson in camouflage.

The rules weren't written down anywhere, but they were everywhere. In my father's scoff at the evening news footage of a Pride parade. In my uncle's laughter when he called me "sissy boy" at a family barbecue. In the way other boys drew hearts next to girls' names, and how I copied them not from feeling, but from fear of being different.

Visibility is dangerous. This became my first commandment.

THE CHURCH OF SILENT SUFFERING

Sunday mornings meant stained glass windows casting colored light across wooden pews, hymns rising like prayers, and the constant weight of being measured against impossible standards. Faith wasn't new or optional for me, it was the foundation everything else was built on.

I loved those quiet moments when the light hit just right and the music swelled. There was something sacred in the silence between songs, something that made me feel seen by something larger than the small town that seemed to be cataloguing my every gesture.

But alongside the hymns came harder lessons. Sermons about the "natural order" of things. Youth group discussions about purity and purpose. Slowly, quietly, I began to understand that the part of me that felt most natural was the part they called unnatural.

I prayed to be fixed. Fasted. Read scripture until my eyes burned. I bargained with God in ways that would break my heart if I heard a child making those same desperate deals today.

Please make me normal. Please take this away. Please let me be what everyone needs me to be.

But some prayers aren't meant to be answered. Some prayers are meant to teach us that we were never broken to begin with.

LEARNING TO PERFORM LOVE

High school brought new stages and more complex performances. I learned to look at girls the way my friends did, even when I felt nothing. I laughed at jokes that made my stomach turn. I dated because it was expected, treating each relationship like a script I had to memorize.

Barbra was my first girlfriend. Kind, patient, everything a teenage boy was supposed to want. She deserved someone who could love her completely, not someone practicing how to fake it convincingly. But I was seventeen and terrified, more afraid of being discovered than of being dishonest.

The relationship lasted six months. When it ended, people asked what went wrong. I shrugged and said we were better as friends, which was true but not complete. The complete truth that I had never felt for her what she deserved to be felt was too dangerous to speak.

Those early years didn't just teach me how to perform. They taught me how to disappear.

Not all at once. Not dramatically. But slowly, like erosion. A soft, steady wearing down of natural instinct. I stopped moving freely. I stopped speaking boldly. I stopped trusting the parts of myself that felt natural but were labeled "wrong."

I became hyper-aware of my body how it moved, how it was perceived, how it betrayed me. I learned to scan every room for danger: a glance too long, a laugh too loud, a question asked with too much curiosity. I learned to anticipate judgment before it arrived.

And I internalized it.

I started to believe that being different meant being defective. That softness was weakness. That joy had to be rationed. I didn't just fear rejection, I expected it. I carried shame like a second skin, invisible but suffocating.

Even in moments of safety, I couldn't fully exhale. Because safety felt temporary. Conditional. Like a gift that could be revoked if I slipped, if I forgot the script, if I let the truth show.

I became a master of adaptation. I could mirror the boys around me, mimic their interests, echo their language. I could laugh at jokes that made me flinch. I could nod along to stories that made me ache. I could be what they needed me to be.

But I couldn't be me.

And that kind of loneliness the kind that comes not from isolation, but from self-erasure is hard to name. It's quiet. It's constant. It's the ache of being surrounded and unseen.

Those years planted seeds. Not just of shame, but of resilience. Because even as I shrank, some part of me held on. Some part of me whispered, "There's more than this." And eventually, I listened.

So, I became a student of performance, a master of mimicry. I learned how to look at girls the way my friends did, even if I felt nothing. I laughed at the jokes that made my stomach twist. I watched my posture, my pitch, and my presence. I played the role so well that I sometimes fooled myself. But the ache never left. It stayed hidden, like a splinter beneath skin. A constant, quiet pain. Not loud enough to scream, but always there.

No one tells you what it costs to live a lie. It costs sleep, laughter, and the ability to look in the mirror and feel at home.

And when you grow up performing safety, pretending to be what the world deems "normal," the applause feels more like chains. Every compliment on being "such a good guy," every moment someone said, "You've got it all, " made the ache deeper. Because I knew they didn't really see me. They saw a version of me. A shadow.

The cruelest thing? No, most of them weren't trying to hurt me, my parents, my teachers, my friends. They didn't hate me. But their love came with unspoken terms: Love the mask. Fear the man beneath it.

And me? I was terrified. Terrified that if I showed who I was, I would stop pretending they'd walk away.

A unique kind of grief comes from being misunderstood while surrounded by people who think they know you. You're at the table, laughing, eating, existing. And still completely alone.

That's what I carried for years. The dissonance. The double life. The constant rehearsal of every interaction. I need to monitor how I walk, how I speak, and how I look. Would this shirt make them guess? Would that word give me away?

It wasn't just about hiding who I loved. It was about hiding *how* I loved, how deeply, how differently, how vulnerable. And still, for years, I convinced myself it was worth it. Because what's the alternative? Rejection? Isolation? Starting over?

I buried my truth so deep that it stopped screaming and started whispering. And then one day, it stopped making noise at all. Or so I thought. But truth doesn't die. It waits. It waits for quiet moments. For breakdowns. For new beginnings. It waits in your breath, heartbeat, and the tears you won't let fall.

And eventually, it rises.

For me, it rose slowly. A question here. A moment there. It took years for the fog to lift. For the shame to loosen. For the first whisper of freedom to reach me. And when it did, it didn't feel like a victory. It felt like grief. Because I realized how much time I'd lost. How many moments I'd lived as a ghost in my own body.

But this chapter isn't about regret. It's about recognition. It's about honoring the boy who tried so hard to be loved that he almost disappeared. It's about holding space for the man who finally said, "No more."

Because now? Now I don't walk into rooms wondering if people will approve of me. I walk in, hoping they will meet me… The real me… No edits… No performance. Just Tedd.

And if you've ever found yourself hiding or smiled through a scream, this chapter is for you, too. We deserve more than survival. We deserve to be known. And that's what this book is about…

It's not about regret.
It's not even about coming out.
It's about that *first quiet ache.*
The one that tells you: *this life looks right, but it doesn't feel right.*

It's recognizing that something is off, not because the world is telling you, but because your soul won't stop whispering.

It's the moment you start to question:

What if I'm not the broken one?
What if the story I was handed… was never mine.

I was becoming fluent in partial truths, expert in the grammar of concealment.

CHAPTER 2

THE PRICE OF ACCEPTANCE

There was always something sacred about silence. As a child, I found that quiet space in church pews where the light hit the stained glass just right, where hymns rose and fell like breath, and where I could even briefly believe that I was seen by something holy. Religion wasn't a routine for me; it was a lifeline. A deep, unwavering belief that I was created intentionally. Loved. Guided.

But as I grew older, I heard another voice rise inside those sacred walls, a colder, sharper one. It claimed that I would fall out of grace unless I walked the straight path. It didn't scream or accuse. It whispered. And I listened.

The tension began like a barely noticeable hairline crack in glass. But the more I tried to align with what was expected, the more that fracture spread across every corner of me. I prayed, fasted, read scripture, and pleaded with God to fix whatever was "wrong" with me.

And then… I rebelled in silence.

Secret experimentation became my outlet. Drugs. Secret encounters with boys. I never dated the girls who called me their best friend. I didn't know how to explain why. I couldn't explain why.

The church youth group I joined during high school offered warmth and belonging. People there cheered for me. They told me I had promise, that I was "going places." But it was never the real me they were seeing; it was the polished, acceptable mask I wore, the boy who could speak scripture with sincerity, smiled through the ache, and belonged… as long as he stayed silent.

COLLEGE: CHOOSING THE CAGE

The acceptance letter from the state university sat on my desk for weeks. Everything I had worked for, everything I had dreamed about, reduced to a thin envelope that felt impossibly heavy in my hands.

But there were other voices. Church leaders who spoke of a "better path." A small Christian college in Indiana where I could "grow my faith" and become "who I was meant to be." The pressure wasn't cruel, it was loving, which made it harder to resist.

Maybe they're right, I thought. *Maybe this place will save me from myself.*

So, I chose the cage, convincing myself it was a sanctuary.

Indiana was beautiful in its own way. Rolling hills, brick buildings, the kind of campus where everyone knew everyone and faith was as much a part of the curriculum as math or literature. I threw myself into college life with the enthusiasm of someone trying to outrun his own shadow.

I worked as a lifeguard at the natatorium, teaching swimming to kids who shrieked with delight when they conquered their fear of deep water. In that chlorinated world, I found something close to peace. The pool was honest either you could swim or you couldn't. There was no performance required, just competence and care.

Dorm life was a slow-burn torment. Handsome men, towel-clad and effortless, walked past me daily. Showers with open stalls. Late-night conversations in shared rooms.

The Friend I Couldn't Name

It was there I met him my teammate, my best friend, the person who would one day stand beside me as best man at my wedding. We were competitive in the water, compatible everywhere else. Same social club, same morning routines, same easy friendship that felt like the most natural thing in the world.

I told myself it was admiration. He was everything I wanted to be: confident, magnetic, effortlessly himself. We trained together, studied together, shared the easy intimacy of close friends. When our group took a weekend trip to California, I watched him under golden coastal light, sand in his hair and laughter in his voice, and felt something shift inside me.

It wasn't admiration. It was love.

The realization terrified me. This was exactly what I had come to Indiana to escape, and here it was, dressed up as friendship, making a home in my carefully guarded heart.

I buried it. Added another layer to the performance, another room to the house of mirrors I was building around my true self. But love doesn't disappear just because you refuse to name it. It goes underground, where it either dies or learns to grow in darkness.

MINISTRY AS ARMOR

After college, ministry felt like destiny. I had a gift for speaking, for connecting with people, for making them feel seen and understood. The irony wasn't lost on me even then I was helping others find their truth while running from my own.

I became good at it. Better than good. People respected me, trusted me, looked to me for guidance. I wore the success like armor, each compliment another layer of protection against the questions I couldn't answer about myself.

But armor is heavy, and after a while, it starts to crush the very thing it was meant to protect.

The breaking point came during a conversation with my mentor, a seminary professor I had trusted with pieces of my struggle. Not the whole truth, I wasn't that brave but enough to hope for understanding.

"Get your act together," he said, his voice cold in a way I had never heard before. "Resist this unhealthy behavior."

No grace. No questions. Just rejection wrapped in religious language.

That night, I sat in my car outside his house, the same house where I had shared countless meals, where his family had welcomed me like a son and felt the last piece of my faith-based identity crack and fall away.

Within weeks, I was quietly asked to step down. To relinquish my credentials. To walk away from the only world where I had felt I belonged.

And so I did, carrying my shame like a secret, telling myself it was temporary. That I would find my way back somehow.

I never did.

CHAPTER 3

THE CORPORATE CLOSET

With shame in my pocket and a young family to support, I pivoted myself to something safe: Human Resources. I told myself it was a temporary job, just something to stabilize. But it became a career, a world of business casual, performance evaluations, and beige-walled comfort.

REINVENTION AS SURVIVAL

Human Resources wasn't a calling it was camouflage. After the ministry collapsed, I needed somewhere to disappear, somewhere I could blend in long enough to figure out what came next.

The corporate world had different rules but the same underlying message: conform or be cast out. I learned the language quickly. Business casual became my new vestments, quarterly reports my new sermons.

In this new environment, identity became a game of survival. I played the role well. I had a deep voice, the tie was loosened just enough, and I chuckled politely when someone mentioned their wife. I even rehearsed my responses to dreaded questions: "How's your family back home?" "What does your wife do?"

Each answer chipped away at something essential.

I played the role of the competent professional, the family man, the safe choice for promotion and it worked. Success came in measured doses raises, recognition, corner offices with views I never had time to appreciate. And the higher I climbed, the more afraid I became. Every step up the ladder was shadowed by a growing terror that one misstep would send it all crashing down. I'd already lost everything once. I couldn't bear to do it again.

From the outside, I had rebuilt perfectly. However, fear wrapped itself around every ambition, every smile, every meeting. And I let it.

The sound of my shoes on marble echoed down the hallway of the corporate office like it always did, confident, clipped, rehearsed. I walked with my shoulders back, my chin up, holding the weight of everything I wasn't allowed to say beneath a starched white shirt and a custom navy blazer.

To the outside world, I was the picture of success. But something was fraying inside.

Inside, I was vanishing.

THE GEOGRAPHY OF FREEDOM

Work took me traveling first across the country, then across oceans. In airport lounges and client dinners, I began to notice something I had never seen at home: people living freely.

One Saturday morning, while sitting in a Barcelona café, I watched a queer couple laugh over croissants. I didn't just envy them, I observed them. Everything about their interaction was effortless, free from caution. Even the way they dressed told a story of ease and ownership.

In Paris, love was worn like jewelry visible, celebrated, unashamed. In Amsterdam, I watched a gay couple laugh over coffee, their ease so complete it looked like a different species of human being. Everything and everyone seemed so normal.

After experiencing this several times over a few years, something shifted inside me. I began to wonder if this could be me. I started to imagine my life differently and soon followed with a simple change in dress. I wore a shirt that fit tighter. I smiled wider. For just a moment, I imagined a life that didn't revolve around hiding.

At first, I was envious. Then curious. Then haunted.

Could that be real? Could someone like me be seen wholly and still succeed? I wasn't ready to answer that. Not yet. But I couldn't unsee it.

Back home, the questions followed me. I needed a release. I created a private file, hidden behind layers of anonymity, where I began to write my truth not to be read, just to be real. Each word peeled back decades of silence, and with each post, I realized: honesty isn't a sin. It's survival.

For the first time in my adult life, I began to wonder if what I had been chasing all along wasn't just success but wholeness.

A life not built on denial, but on truth. A voice not buried in silence, but heard fully, fearlessly.

I was not ready to step into that vision yet. But I saw it. And that vision refused to let go, no matter how fragile or terrifying.

I often thought about how far we've come as humans, as a civilization, as living, breathing beings trying to make sense of the world we're born into.

Our ancestors fought for shelter, fire, and food when the world was a scattered wilderness. That was survival. Centuries later, they fought for the right to speak freely, to cast a vote, to be free from the chains of slavery. Our great-grandparents marched, bled, and broke to give us what we now call "freedom." In return, at least we inherited an easier life on the surface.

We live in an age where everything is just a tap away. Groceries are delivered. Lights are voice-controlled. Love swipes are possible. Luxury, technology, and convenience all paint this illusion of a perfect world. But beneath it, the one thing that hasn't evolved with the same speed… is our emotional freedom.

These weren't just observations, they were revelations. For the first time, I saw that the life I thought was impossible wasn't just possible, it was happening everywhere I looked.

But seeing freedom isn't the same as claiming it.

I had learned to compartmentalize, to hide my truth under board reports and quarterly reviews. I kept it buried beneath leadership and charm, beneath husband and father, beneath God and community. I wore my role like a tailored suit, polished, perfected, suffocating.

Then one afternoon, in a quiet conference room, I cracked.

We were alone, me and a colleague I thought I could trust. I don't even remember what led up to it. Maybe a conversation about families. Or loneliness. But the words came out like steam from a pressure valve.

"I'm tired of pretending," I said. "There's more to me than this job, this box I'm supposed to live in." He didn't say much. Just nodded. But something shifted. The room felt colder after that. The following week, my calendar was emptier with fewer invites. Polite avoidance. Not long after, I was asked to step down. The reason? "We're moving in a different direction." I knew what that meant. I had let my truth leak through the seams, and truth was a liability in that world.

THE DOUBLE LIFE

But I didn't fall apart. I pivoted. I had become an expert of rebounding over the years. So I found a business in Florida and bought it, once again starting over.

Florida started as a business opportunity. A company to acquire, a market to enter, a practical decision that made sense on paper.

My wife didn't want to move because the kids had friends, we had a life, she said. But I pushed, though I couldn't explain why, even to myself. The move made sense on paper, the weather, the opportunity, the market, but looking back, I wonder if deep down she sensed what Florida might awaken in me. And maybe... I did too. So, I moved to Fort Lauderdale.

Fort Lauderdale was heat and possibility, palm trees and rainbow flags flying without apology. Just twenty minutes away, Wilton Manors pulsed with a kind of life I had only imagined men holding hands in broad daylight, laughter that didn't carry the weight of caution, joy that didn't require permission.

The first time I walked into a bar there, I wasn't looking for anything specific. I told myself I was just curious, just observing. But when I sat at the counter and looked around, I saw something that stopped my breath: men like me. Not just gay but layered. Men with stories behind their eyes, men who had worn masks too. As I sat there, I recognized I felt something genuine inside of me as I looked at all these men. It wasn't lust I felt, it was the sense that I too could be recognized as the person I was created to be.

But truth has its own weight. And eventually, even the strongest person can't carry it alone.

I lived between two selves, like a man straddling two boats slowly drifting apart. My boys were in Jr High and High School by this time. Regularly, I flew home for their activities. And then I returned to a place where I could breathe without hiding my heartbeat. But with every return, the mask felt heavier.

There is a passage by James Baldwin that always stopped me cold: "Love takes off the masks we fear we cannot live without and know we cannot live within."

That was me. I had built a life around a mask so complete, even though I had forgotten it was there. Coming out wasn't just about attraction. It was about authenticity. About reclaiming a voice, I had muted for decades.

Still, the conflict wasn't as simple as a binary switch. I didn't wake up one morning and say, "I'm gay" and watch my life rearrange itself. I said it softly, in stages, sometimes only to myself. I questioned it even as I tried to own it. Because who was I now? A gay man? A father? A man who still loved the woman he had built a life with, even if that love had changed its shape?

And then came the fatigue, not the kind that sleep can fix, but the ache of emotional dissonance, the tug-of-war between being known and being safe, belonging and betraying. My body felt it first: the heaviness in my chest, the way I had to coach myself to smile sometimes, the weight of pretending not to be torn in two.

Yet I never missed a game or important event. Never forgot a birthday. My kids didn't get half of me. They got all of me. But so did my version of learning to dance in the dim light of Wilton's late evenings.

And somewhere between those two selves, I began to wonder: Was it possible that both were real? That maybe I wasn't betraying one life, but finally learning to integrate them?

And loneliness, God, the loneliness.

Not from lack of people. But from the lack of *being known*. In one world, I hid the part of me that loved a man. In the other, I was burying the part that had once loved a woman. Both parts were genuine. Both deserved breaths. And yet, neither felt safe.

This is where society fails all of us. Not just gay people. Not just men like me. But *everyone*. Because the world doesn't make space for complexity, it hands us molds Father. Husband. Wife. Executive. Straight. Gay. And says, *fit into this or you're broken*. So, we shape ourselves to survive. We shave off edges. We smile when we want to scream. We say *"I'm fine"* even when something inside us quietly dies.

But at some point, you have to decide: do I keep twisting myself to fit a story that was never mine, or do I write a new one?

That question haunted me not in loud moments, but in the soft ones, in the spaces between my kids' laughter, in the hush of closing my laptop, in the way my heart clenched every time I watched someone live freely while I tiptoed around my own truth.

And still, I didn't choose. Not yet.

I kept living in the in-between, not because I was weak but because I was still healing. I needed time, grace, and to believe that there was a way to be *whole* without needing to be *perfect*.

So I stayed in motion, coaching soccer games, running team meetings, sipping coffee at LGBTQ cafés, pretending I belonged everywhere and nowhere. It was messy. It was real.

And maybe, just maybe, it was enough for now.

A FINAL NOTE FROM THE HEART......

If you've ever walked into a room and left
part of yourself at the door...
If you've ever questioned whether your truth
was too heavy, different, or complicated...
If you've ever been made to feel that love had to come in a
specific shape, or that freedom came only after you earned it...

Then this book is for you.

And maybe, like me, you're still figuring it out.

So, I offer you this.

Not as closure, but as a company:

"They called it confusion....
But it was just me, learning to name every color of my soul."

Even the oldest stories began in verse. Maybe that's because when language fails us, rhythm remembers. And in this rhythm, I hope you find yourself.

Too often, we confuse emotional awareness with fragility. But the truth is, it takes immense strength to sit with your pain, to speak your truth out loud, to stand in a room and say: *This is who I am. And I am not ashamed.*

I'm not just speaking for myself. I'm speaking for every person who's had to dim their light to fit in. For the kid who was told to "man up" when he cried. For the girl who wanted to lead but was called bossy. For the boy who loved pink and was laughed at. For the woman who chose not to marry and got labeled broken. For the queer teen whose closet was built by other people's shame. For the ones still trying to breathe inside cages made by culture and tradition.

We carry these invisible bruises given to us not by fists, but by ideas. Stereotypes.

Someone once told me, "Your truth is too loud." But I think the world needs to hear not just mine but all of ours. The truths that make people uncomfortable are often the ones that need to be spoken the most.

That's why I write this. That's why I tell this story not just for the LGBTQ community, but for every soul quietly suffocating under labels they didn't choose. This isn't a "gay" story. This is a human story. One about reclaiming the right to feel. To love. To cry. To belong.

And to anyone who feels alone right now, I see you.

No matter who you are or where you come from, you deserve space. You don't have to earn it. You were born with it.

Let's build a world where softness isn't shameful, boundaries are respected, labels are peeled away, and truth remains. Let's hold space for one another. Let's choose compassion over cruelty. And above all… let's not be afraid to feel.

Because to feel is not a flaw.

It's our greatest strength.

CHAPTER 4

WHEN THE BODY KEEPS SCORE

THE NIGHTS I COULDN'T SLEEP

By my forties, I was the image of success. The office with a view, the framed degrees on the wall, the pictures of smiling children on my desk. My wife, everything I once thought I needed, stood proudly beside me at business functions, fundraisers, and family gatherings. People smiled when they saw us. And I smiled back.

But there were nights I couldn't sleep.

Nights when the silence grew too thick and the stillness too loud. I'd lie restless in bed, wondering how I had ended up inside a life that looked perfect from the outside but felt like it was slowly erasing me. I had built everything with discipline, structure, and intention: marriage, kids, promotions, respectability. The ring on my finger, the glass of vodka always nearby, the steady rhythm of achievement. Every polished milestone added another layer of gloss over a growing crack I dared not name.

There was no obvious breaking point. No scandal, no betrayal, no secret storm. Just the slow, persistent ache of pretending.

Some days, I caught myself glancing too long at strangers not out of lust, but out of longing. Longing for the freedom they seemed to carry so effortlessly. How they moved through the world unhidden, unedited, made me ache with recognition. It wasn't that I wanted to be them. I wanted to be free like them.

I told myself I had everything I needed. But the truth was sharper than my excuses: I was performing. At home, I played the role of the engaged husband, the loving father. At work, I was the problem solver, the leader, the polished professional. In every space, I felt like I was disappearing, one careful gesture at a time.

The applause never reached my core. The compliments echoed back hollow. Even intimacy became routine something to schedule, complete, and maintain for appearances.

People said I was "living the dream." But no one ever asked if it was mine. And if they had, I wouldn't have known how to answer.

THE DOUBLE LIFE

Wilton Manors had become more than a destination it was a window into who I might be. What started as exploration quickly evolved into a double existence, as carefully orchestrated as any corporate merger. When I was there, I didn't have to overthink my gestures or calculate my words. I could laugh without measuring the volume. I could breathe without holding space for someone else's comfort. But then I'd return to Ohio and put the mask back on. And every time I did, it got heavier.

At first, I convinced myself it was manageable. I had orchestrated my compartmentalized life with such precision that I believed it could run like a well-oiled machine. Ohio was the stage, Florida the sanctuary. One life to be admired, the other to be inhaled quietly, like stolen air.

But even steel eventually bends under persistent heat.

It started with minor slips a name spoken too casually, a lingering glance across a crowded room, the way my body relaxed when certain songs played. The distance between Wilton Manors and Ohio school gymnasiums didn't seem so vast anymore.

I told myself I was protecting everyone: my wife, my children, even the men I loved in quiet moments. But really, I was shielding the most fragile part of me, the version that couldn't bear the cost of exposure.

Compartmentalization is a clever lie you tell yourself when you believe the walls are strong enough to carry the weight. But they're not. They hold just long enough to trap you inside.

Still, I kept performing. I was at every parent-teacher conference, clapping at soccer games, nodding at church services. I slipped back into the straight husband character with practiced ease. It was my most rehearsed role.

But in Florida, the edges of my mask began to fray. There, I allowed myself to unravel. The friendships ran deeper, warmer. I could speak in complete sentences instead of code. I laughed louder, breathed easier, kissed without consequence or calculation.

THE BREAKING POINT

It was a Saturday morning in August, golden Florida light streaming through the windows. I had just returned from a long bike ride training for a triathlon because even in my double life, I needed goals to chase, mountains to climb, ways to prove I was still in control.

My boyfriend who I met in Dallas while on a business trip months earlier, known only in Florida, never mentioned in Ohio, was waiting when I walked through the door, salt-stained and endorphin-high.

"Coffee?" he asked, our code for the ritual trip to Dunkin' Donuts.

"Yeah," I said, wiping sweat from my neck. "Let me shower first. Ten minutes."

We rode bikes to the local Dunkin' him waiting outside to secure the bikes while I went in to order our usual. But when he joined me at the counter, I couldn't speak. The words jumbled in my mouth, and then the pain hit, sharp and stealing, radiating down my arm like electricity.

"Call 911," I managed to whisper, and he understood immediately.

The ER doctor didn't waste time with gentle language. "You're having an aortic event," he said, the words hitting like cold water. "A tear in your main artery. Call anyone who matters. Now."

In that sterile room, with monitors beeping and the smell of antiseptic thick in the air, I told my boyfriend everything for the first time. About Ohio. About the family waiting there. About the life I had built on careful omissions and strategic truths.

Then I called my wife.

"Don't come yet," I told her through the pain and medication. "Wait until after the surgery. I need to survive first."

It was the first completely honest thing I had said in years, even if only to myself.

RECOVERY AND RECKONING

The surgery saved my life, but in doing so, it quietly rewrote everything. For days, I lay still, hooked to machines monitoring every heartbeat while the compartments I'd spent decades building collapsed in silence around me.

My wife flew down, still unaware of the full picture, still kind and tender, smoothing hospital blankets and holding my hand with the devotion of someone who believed in the life we had built together. Her love felt like both a gift and an indictment.

When I was stable enough, we returned to Ohio. "We'll take care of you," she said, and I let her, because I didn't know how to explain that the person she was caring for was only half of who I really was.

Back home, I tried to resume the performance. But something fundamental had shifted. The near-death experience had cracked something open that couldn't be sealed again. Recovery wasn't just about healing my body, it was about facing what my body had been trying to tell me all along.

You can't keep living this way.

THE PHOTOGRAPH

Several months passed. I tried to slip back into old patterns, but I couldn't perform with the same conviction. She noticed something different about me but couldn't name what had changed. In searching for answers, she went through my belongings and found a photograph in my wallet, one that didn't fit the script she thought we were still writing together.

She held it up without words. I didn't deny it. I couldn't. I simply breathed out the truth I'd been holding for decades.

"I need to tell you everything."

And finally, after a lifetime of carefully constructed performances, I did.

The world I had built in Ohio disintegrated in that moment. But I didn't realize that my sanctuary in Florida was crumbling too. Word travels fast in small communities. Friends became aware of the double life I'd been living. Whispers turned into conversations. Some pulled away. Wilton Manors no longer offered the unconditional safety it once had.

Everything I thought I was balancing lay in debris around me.

But for the first time in my adult life, I was standing in the wreckage as myself.

THE LONG WALK FORWARD

Coming out wasn't a finish line, it was mile one of a different marathon.

In the quiet that followed the revelations, I sat with questions I had never dared to ask:

> *Why am I merely surviving instead of living?*
> *How long will I pretend just to be loved?*
> *How much of my soul will I trade for acceptance?*

I started therapy. I cried in rooms I used to command with corporate confidence. I let go of the illusion of control. I tried to parent not as a performer playing a role, but as a flawed, honest human being. Some days I succeeded. Others, I faltered completely.

But I showed up. I kept showing up.

I think of people like Colton Haynes, the actor whose career once required a straight mask until his truth broke through the carefully constructed facade. Or poet Ocean Vuong, who writes about identity with the softness of rain and the sharpness of glass. Like me, they didn't choose their truths, truth isn't a choice. But they chose not to run from it forever.

And so, I walk forward, not perfectly, but honestly. I lost the applause, the easy approval, the comfort of fitting in. But I gained something more valuable: my own echo, my own voice calling back from the canyon of authenticity.

THE UNIVERSAL ACHE

It's tempting to assume that stories like mine belong only to those who walk society's margins, those born into identities that don't quite fit the prescribed molds. But the more I reflect, the more I understand this isn't just my story, it's a mirror reflecting something larger, more universal.

The details differ for each of us, but the ache remains constant: the pressure, the silent rules of who we're supposed to be, the weight of living up to expectations that were never truly ours.

We're all raised in systems that dictate how to look, how to behave, who to love, what success should mean. From birth, expectations wrap around us like invisible threads. Some of us feel the constriction sooner than others. For me, it was sexual identity. For others, it might be career choices, faith, gender expression, mental health, physical appearance, or simply the volume at which they're allowed to speak their truth.

I've witnessed this pressure crush people who were never part of any marginalized community. The straight, married man who quietly battles depression because he's not "allowed" to say he's drowning. The young woman told to smile, shrink, and agree until she forgets her own opinions. The immigrant made to feel perpetually foreign. The boy taught that real men don't cry, don't falter, don't ask for help.

Different stories. Same undertow.

Our society treats pain like a competition, as if some people deserve to suffer more or less based on their position in the social hierarchy. But listen closely to anyone's story, and you'll hear the tremor when they speak of their youth, the moment they were made to feel wrong, insufficient, or excessive. The moment they stopped feeling safe just being themselves.

People say, "At least things are better now. People are more accepting." And perhaps some things appear better on the surface rainbow logos in June, mental health hashtags, corporate diversity statements. But underneath, so many of us are still struggling to simply *be*, still healing from wounds no one ever acknowledged, let alone apologized for.

WHAT WE DO NOW

We start by seeing each other not through categories, assumptions, or political divides, but through our shared fragility, through the moments we've all felt diminished. We stop asking "Who has it worse?" and start asking "How can I understand you better?"

We remember that someone can appear successful, conventional, and comfortable from the outside while breaking apart internally. We recognize that the straight, cisgender, financially secure person sitting next to us might be drowning in expectations just as suffocating as any closet.

I used to think my identity made me fundamentally different. In some ways, it does. But in the ways that matter most, the need to be seen, to be accepted, to belong, it simply makes me human.

And that's something we all share.

We are not as separate as we think. We are not as alone as we feel.

The first language of pain was poetry, not to beautify suffering, but to speak what silence never could. If you've ever held your breath to fit in, if you've ever performed your life instead of living it, maybe it's time to exhale.

I finally did. And in that breath, I found not just my voice, but my life.

CHAPTER 5

THE UNRAVELING

When Truth Becomes Earthquake

I enjoyed being with my wife. Her laughter could soften the sharpest moments. She was the first person I'd turn to when the world felt too loud, too cruel. I loved her, but my heart didn't pulse with romance. It rested with her in calm companionship, not wild desire. Ours was love rooted in understanding, not in longing. A love that offered comfort but never called to the deepest corners of me.

The world I had built in Ohio didn't collapse dramatically it unraveled thread by thread, like a sweater with one pulled string.

My wife's reaction moved through stages. First shock, then the desperate hope that this was temporary, fixable. She researched support groups for men "dealing with same-sex attraction," left pamphlets on the counter, suggested therapy that could "help me through this phase."

I tried to go along with it at first. Made a few calls, spoke to counselors who assured me I was sick but curable. Their voices echoed everything I had been told as a child, everything I had spent years in therapy trying to unlearn.

But I couldn't unknow what I had learned about myself. I couldn't go back to the cage, even a comfortable one.

When she realized, I wasn't going to comply, wasn't going to "recover", her patience gave way to something harder. Our conversations became negotiations, then arguments, then cold calculations about assets and who would get what in the wreckage.

THE COST OF COMING OUT

My sons took the news differently.

When I told them individually. I was surprised by their initial calm. There was something in their eyes not judgment, but sadness. Maybe they had known on some level, the way children sometimes understand things adults think they're hiding.

"I still love you, Dad," my youngest said, and for a moment, I believed that love might be enough to bridge any distance.

But life doesn't unfold in neat emotional arcs.

My oldest son called me during the divorce proceedings, his voice tight with anger and grief. "If you ever want a relationship with me and my family, or to see your grandchildren, you better be good to Mom in the divorce settlement."

I agreed to everything he asked. Gave more than was required, hoping generosity might buy back their respect. But even then, I lost him. Some bridges can't be rebuilt with good intentions.

My youngest kept reaching out for a while. He visited Georga, met my partner, shared dinners where laughter came easily. For precious months, I let myself believe that maybe, with time, we could find our way back to each other.

Then the silence started. Not angry, just absent. No explanation, no gradual fade. Just the terrible quiet that follows when someone decides you no longer exist in their story.

And my boys… they were the brightest light in my world. Sparks of life and wonder, arms always reaching, eyes always asking. They filled the space with energy, and my heart with a quiet awe. I adored them with everything I had. They were joy, in motion. But even joy, when unaccompanied by truth, becomes a distraction rather than a balm.

Between the laughter and bedtime rituals, the celebrations and the small victories, I felt gratitude, but not authenticity. I wore the mask of contentment convincingly, but it didn't fit. joy was present, yet it never pierced deep enough to reach the part of me still searching.

And so, I kept running. Not just through city streets and mountain trails, but away from the quiet emptiness that flickered between moments of good. Love surrounded me. Joy bloomed around me. But neither could answer the ache that whispered: This isn't who you truly are.

It's a strange thing, to be surrounded by love and still feel empty. To tuck your child in with a kiss and then retreat to the bathroom mirror, searching your own eyes for some proof that you belong in the life you've built. I gave them everything I had,

Devotion, Time. My best attempts at presence. But there was always a part of me standing just outside the frame… Always a voice whispering, *if they really knew you…*

It wasn't about not loving them; I loved them fiercely. But I didn't know how to love myself. I feared that my authenticity was dangerous, that showing the real me would upend the home I had spent years carefully constructing. So, I lived as two people. The husband. The father. Roles I cherished, but ones I performed. And then, the quiet self I buried. The one who wondered what it might be like to be loved as-is not despite what I hid, but because of who I was.

And when the house grew quiet and the dishes were washed, when another race medal hung forgotten on the wall, I was left with a silence that didn't feel like peace. I was left with a stranger in the mirror.

Sometimes when I was alone in my new home, I imagine what it would be like to speak my truth out loud. To say, *I'm tired of pretending. I want to be loved in the raw, not the polished.* But fear always pulled me back. What if honesty unraveled it all? What if naming the ache destroyed everything it had helped build?

So, I stayed quiet. And kept giving. And sometimes, that felt noble. Other times, it felt like slow erasure.

If I could have asked for anything during those years, it wouldn't have been understanding. It would have been courage. The courage to believe that being fully known didn't mean being left behind. The courage to trust that my story with its messy edges and hidden chapters still deserved a place in the open.

THE COMMUNITY THAT COULDN'T HOLD ME

I expected to lose some friends, the ones whose love was conditional, whose comfort required my conformity. What I didn't expect was how hard it would be to find my place in the community I thought would welcome me.

Coming out gave me language but not belonging. I had the words, gay, queer, authentic, but I still felt like I was translating myself for every conversation. The men I met in Wilton Manors had stories like mine but different rhythms. They had learned to be themselves years earlier, or had never learned to hide as completely as I had.

I was forty-something and learning to be gay like a teenager learns to drive, tentatively, with too much attention to the rules, aware that everyone else seems to navigate this territory with an ease I couldn't find.

There's a closet within the closet, I discovered. The place you retreat to when even your authentic self doesn't feel quite right, when freedom still requires translation, when you're out but not yet home.

The tragedy of that time wasn't just the lie. It was that I gave so much love away without ever believing I was worthy of receiving it back. Not fully. Not truthfully.

And yet, somewhere between the parties I planned and the finish lines I crossed, I began to see the pattern, not of healing, but of hiding. Every event, every moment of distraction, was another brick in a wall around me. I mistook productivity for progress. The busyness, the constant motion, it felt like life. But it wasn't living. It was surviving. It was avoiding.

It's funny how exhaustion can masquerade as accomplishment. People praised my energy, my dedication, my commitment. But I knew the truth. I had simply become better at hiding emptiness with effort.

This chapter isn't about reproach or sadness from loss.

It's about the ache of unreturned self-love, and the guilt that comes when your heart longs to be known without destroying what it's helped create.

CHAPTER 6

A QUIET REVOLUTION
LEARNING A NEW
LANGUAGE OF LOVE

COMING HOME TO MYSELF

So, I kept running not just through races and routines, but away from the truth sitting in the shadows of my own heart.

The first time I came out, it was quiet. No fireworks. No audience. Just me, in Dallas where no one knew my name. I had slipped away on a business trip and found myself standing outside a gay bar, heart pounding not from fear, but from possibility. I was stepping into a mirror for the first time, hoping to catch a glimpse of myself, not as a father, not as a husband, but simply as *me*.

For once, the reflection didn't flinch. It didn't ask for permission. It simply waited.

That night didn't ask for labels, it asked only for honesty. Inside, I felt a strange calm. No explanations needed. No performances required. It was like walking into the rehearsal of a life I wasn't yet brave enough to claim, but one that finally felt real. Safe. Mine.

But no one tells you you'll have to come out more than once. Coming out isn't an event, it's a practice, as daily and necessary as breathing.

THE WORLD AS MIRROR

My work took me further from home, first across the country, then across oceans. I saw the world through a different lens; one not fogged by fear or the familiar weight of others' expectations. I met people who lived openly, whose identities weren't buried beneath performance. I watched strangers hold hands, laugh without measuring the volume, live without apology. And it cracked something open in me.

The Midwest had taught me silence, not just the kind that fills rooms, but the kind that fills entire lives. It taught me how to smile through discomfort, how to nod through dissonance, how to disappear in plain sight. But the world beyond whispered different truths, inviting me to lean closer to myself.

In Barcelona, I saw love painted across alley walls, graffiti hearts and rainbow flags fluttering from balconies like prayers made visible. Couples kissed in public without hesitation, their joy unedited, their affection requiring no translation. The city pulsed with color and defiance, as if it had decided long ago that shame had no place in its rhythm.

In Paris, love was quieter but no less bold. I watched two men share a bottle of wine beside the Seine, their fingers brushing between sips, their laughter soft but unafraid. There was elegance in their ease, a kind of rebellion wrapped in tenderness. No one stared. No one flinched. It was just life, unfolding naturally.

In Christchurch, I met a gay medical doctor who had transitioned from marriage to living authentically while maintaining loving relationships with his ex-wife and children. "Here, we're small but fierce," he told me. "We don't ask for space, we make it." His words stayed with me. Even in a city bound by tradition, he had carved out joy. Not loud, but lasting.

Each place gave me a new language for freedom not just words, but ways of being. Each city became a mirror, reflecting back parts of myself I hadn't known I was allowed to claim. In Berlin, I found the safety of anonymity. In Mexico City, the joy of being seen without explanation. These weren't just trips, they were experiments in authenticity.

THE ARCHAEOLOGY OF SELF

Therapy became my new practice, not the kind that promises easy answers, but the kind that offers patient excavation, digging through layers of performance to find the person buried beneath.

"Who were you before you learned to be afraid?" my therapist asked during one session.

I couldn't remember. The boy who danced without thinking, who moved through the world without calculating every gesture, felt like a character from someone else's story.

But slowly, carefully, we began to uncover him. In memories of unguarded laughter, in moments of joy that required no audience, in the stubborn persistence of hope even through decades of hiding.

My counselor called my coping mechanisms "adaptive survival" the charm, the perfectionism, the curated self. They weren't character flaws; they were strategies I'd built to earn love in environments that didn't feel safe. But healing begins when safety becomes internalized. With each genuine connection, each moment of being accepted without performance, the armor began to loosen.

I didn't need it anymore.

Each encounter whispered the same message: *You don't have to disappear to be accepted.* This became the reparenting work learning to speak to myself with the compassion I'd long reserved for others. Folding laundry and feeling the weight of invisibility lift. Watching a couple kiss in a film and realizing I didn't need perfect clarity about my identity to know that I mattered. Catching my own reflection and, for once, not turning away.

These were micro-moments of healing, the kind therapists say accumulate into transformation.

THE PERMISSION TO NOT KNOW

Coming out again meant admitting I didn't have all the answers. My therapist called it "tolerating ambiguity." I wasn't definitively gay. I wasn't definitively straight. I wasn't definitively sure about much except that the performance had to end.

And finally, that uncertainty didn't feel like a crisis. It felt like a confession. Like exhaling after holding my breath for too many years. Like stepping into the unknown and realizing it wasn't empty, it was spacious.

I started grieving the versions of myself I had constructed to be loved. Grief work in counseling isn't just about mourning loss; it's about releasing identities we crafted to survive. The witty friend who always had the right joke. The reliable sibling who never caused problems. The charming husband who made everything look effortless. They weren't lies, exactly. They were armor personas stitched together from expectation and fear, worn so long they felt like skin.

But they weren't me.

When I finally laid them down, I braced for shame. I thought the silence would be unbearable. Instead, it felt sacred. Then came peace. Then came freedom.

My therapist once said, "You don't have to be who you were to be loved now." I didn't believe him at first. For so long, love felt conditional, *be funny, be helpful, be agreeable, then maybe you'll be enough.* But healing taught me that love built on performance isn't love at all. It's a transaction.

LEARNING TO LOVE WITHOUT TRANSLATION

The first time I said "I love you" to a man and meant it completely without reservation, without the need to translate it through layers of acceptable explanation I cried. Not from sadness, but from the overwhelming relief of finally speaking in my native emotional language.

Love, I discovered, is different when you're not filtering it through performance. It's immediate, uncomplicated, frightening in its simplicity. There's no script to follow, no role to play, just the terrifying, exhilarating experience of being seen completely and chosen anyway.

But learning to receive that love proved harder than learning to give it. For years, I had believed that being fully known would mean being rejected. When it didn't happen, when someone saw all my complicated history and loved me not despite it but because it had shaped me into who I was, I didn't know how to trust it.

Worthiness is difficult to learn when you've spent decades believing you don't deserve to be loved as you are.

THE FRIENDS WHO STAYED

Not everyone disappeared when I stopped performing. Some friends surprised me with their grace, their capacity to hold complexity without demanding neat resolution. They didn't pretend to understand every aspect of my journey, but they were willing to walk alongside it anyway.

My oldest sister was visiting me in Florida. She met my boyfriend, who I presented as a business associate. When he left for a few minutes, she asked me if I was gay and he was my partner and I said yes. Her response was, "I've known since you were young," laughter warming her voice. "I was just waiting for you to catch up."

These relationships built not on who I had pretended to be but on who I actually was felt fundamentally different. Lighter. More real. Conversations didn't require careful translation anymore. Laughter didn't need to be calculated. Presence didn't need to be performed.

I learned the difference between being loved and being known. I had been loved for years, but always with invisible asterisks, always with the unspoken understanding that certain parts of me would remain hidden. Being known fully, completely, without reservation was an entirely different kind of gift.

The Universal Journey Home

I didn't come out to the world so much as I came home to myself. And that, I've come to believe, is the most radical act available to any of us.

Because once you tell yourself the truth, once you stop hiding from your own gaze, the world loses much of its power to define you. You stop asking for permission to exist. You stop negotiating your worth based on others' comfort levels. You start living.

This journey isn't unique to sexual identity. It's the same path walked by anyone who has ever felt the weight of living someone else's expectations. The woman who finally admits she doesn't want children. The man who leaves the family business to become an artist. The person who stops pretending their mental health struggles don't exist. The individual who finally says they don't believe what they were raised to believe.

Different details. Same courage required.

We all have parts of ourselves we've learned to hide, aspects of our identity we've been told are too much, too little, too complicated for public consumption. We've all felt the exhaustion that comes from constant translation, from presenting edited versions of ourselves to earn acceptance.

The path home to authenticity is always paved with the same materials: honest self-reflection, the courage to disappoint others in service of our own truth, the willingness to grieve who we thought we had to be, and the radical act of believing we deserve love without conditions.

THE ONGOING PRACTICE

Recovery isn't a destination, it's daily practice. Some days I felt strong, clear, proud of the courage it had taken to claim my truth. Other days I wondered if I had destroyed everything good in my life for the sake of being honest about something I still didn't fully understand about myself.

But that uncertainty no longer feels like failure. It feels like being human.

Therapy didn't hand me answers wrapped in neat bows. It handed me something more valuable: permission. Permission to be uncertain. Permission to be whole. Permission to be free.

So, if you're still hiding, still shape-shifting to be palatable, still translating yourself into more acceptable versions, I see you. I understand the weight you carry, the careful calculations, the exhaustion of constant performance.

And I promise you this: the real you is not too much. The real you is not a burden. The real you is not a problem to be solved or a secret to be kept. The real you is waiting, not for the world to accept you, but for you to accept yourself.

When you do, everything changes. Not because the world gets easier, but because you finally know who you are. And that knowing, that unshakable sense of your own worth, becomes the foundation for everything else.

The mirror stops lying. The performance ends. The real life begins.

And you discover that coming home to yourself was always the destination you were seeking.

CHAPTER 7

THE SILENCE THAT SPEAKS

LETTERS I'LL NEVER SEND

Dear Son,

I dream about you sometimes. In these dreams, you're still small enough to fall asleep on my chest, still young enough to believe I have answers to impossible questions. In these dreams, I never have to explain myself because love doesn't require explanation. We're building sandcastles or throwing a baseball in the backyard, and the world is simple again just a father and his boy, before everything got complicated.

I know you think I chose something over you. That I picked my truth over your comfort, my authenticity over your sense of family. But I need you to understand, I didn't choose to be gay any more than you chose to be straight. I only chose to stop pretending I wasn't.

The man you're angry at, the one who disrupted everything you thought was stable, he's not a different person from the dad who taught you to ride a bike, who cheered at your games, who held you when nightmares made the world too scary. He's the same person, finally honest enough to stop hiding. I'm still the father who worried about you on your first day of school, who felt proud watching you learn to tie your shoes, who would have done anything to protect you from pain except continue lying about who I am.

You were eight when you asked me why some people are different colors. "God likes variety," I told you. "The world would be boring if everyone was the same." I believed that then. I believe it now. But somehow, when it came to love, to identity, to the deepest parts of who we are, I forgot my own lesson.

I would change everything about how this happened if I could. The timing, the chaos, the way your mother found out, the way it all exploded instead of unfolding gently. But I wouldn't change the truth that made it necessary. Because living a lie, no matter how comfortable, no matter how familiar was slowly killing the father you deserved to have.

I love you with every breath I take. I'm proud of the man you're becoming, even from this distance. I'm sorry it took me so long to figure out how to love myself. And I'm sorry that my journey to wholeness felt like abandonment to you.

You don't have to forgive me. You don't have to understand. But please know this: nothing you could ever do or say or become would make me stop being proud to be your father.

Dad

The letter sits in my desk drawer, unfinished and unsent one for each boy. There are dozens like it words I write but don't send, conversations I rehearse but never have, apologies that hang in the air like smoke from a fire that's already burned out.

THE WEIGHT OF LIVING SILENCE

The hardest part of losing my children wasn't the dramatic moments, the arguments, the ultimatums, the doors slamming so hard the pictures rattled on the walls. It was the ordinary silence that followed. The absence of their voices calling to tell me about a promotion, a heartbreak, a funny thing that happened at work. No more random text messages. No more calls just to check in. No longer being included in the small, daily moments that actually make up a relationship.

Christmas became a minefield. Father's Day turned into the loneliest day of the year, not because I wasn't still a father (that bond doesn't break, even when communication does), but because I had no way to express that fatherhood anymore. No one to call, no cards to receive, no shared meals to anchor the day in connection.

I learned to grieve the living. To mourn relationships that still exist but are no longer accessible. To carry love for people who have decided you no longer exist in their story.

It's a specific kind of death watching someone you love choose to act as if you never mattered, as if the years of bedtime stories and scraped-knee kisses and proud moments at school plays were just a fever dream. You find yourself wanting to knock on their door and say, "Remember when you were five and afraid of the monster under your bed? Remember how I checked every night until you felt safe? That father didn't disappear. He's still right here."

But you can't. Because they've decided that the father who loved them was a lie, and the man who told the truth is a stranger.

THE GRANDCHILDREN I'LL NEVER KNOW

My oldest son had children before our relationship ended. For several precious months, I was a grandfather, the role I'd been anticipating since the day he was born. I had plans: fishing trips when they got older, Saturday morning pancakes, being the grandfather who always had time and patience because I'd learned from my mistakes as a father.

Now they exist for me only in photographs posted on social media accounts I shouldn't visit but sometimes do, in the deep hours of the night when missing them becomes unbearable. I watch them grow from a distance, these small people who share my DNA but will never know my stories, never hear me read *Goodnight Moon* in the voice that used to make their father giggle.

I see him in them the way my grandson tilts his head when he's thinking, the way my granddaughter scrunches her nose when she laughs. It's like watching echoes of a life I'm no longer allowed to live.

I wonder what they'll be told about me, if anything. Whether I'll become a cautionary tale whispered between adults, or simply a blank space in their family history. Whether they'll ever be curious enough to seek out their own truth about who I was and why I disappeared from their story.

The legacy I wanted to leave was love, wisdom, presence, the grandfather who showed up, who remembered birthdays, who had endless patience for building block towers and answering impossible questions. Instead, I left confusion and an absence that will shape them in ways I'll never understand.

Sometimes I imagine them as teenagers, asking hard questions: "Why don't we see Grandpa anymore?" "What happened to Dad's father?" And I wonder if anyone will tell them that love comes in different forms, that families can be broken by truth and still hold pieces of beauty.

THE UNIVERSAL ACHE

This grief, the grief of chosen separation, isn't unique to parents whose children reject them for being LGBTQ+. It lives in any parent whose truth became unacceptable to their child. The mother whose daughter can't forgive her for leaving an abusive marriage. The father, whose son refuses contact after a bitter divorce. The parent whose child cuts ties over religious differences, political beliefs, or simply the weight of old hurts that never healed.

It lives in the adoptive parent whose child chooses to reconnect with biological family and disappears from the life that raised them. In the stepparent who loved someone else's child as their own, only to lose that relationship when the marriage ended. In the foster parent who opened their heart to a teen who aged out of the system and decided connection was too risky.

The details differ, but the ache remains constant: loving someone who has decided you are the problem in their story.

LETTERS TO THE UNIVERSE

Dear Daughter I Don't Have,

If you existed, I would tell you that you never have to choose between loving yourself and loving others. I would teach you that authenticity isn't selfish, it's the greatest gift you can give to the people who matter. I would show you how to stand in your truth without apology, because I finally learned how.

Dear Daughter-in-Law,

Take care of my boy. Love him the way I should have shown him love looks without fear, without the need to hide pieces of yourself to be acceptable. Be the example I couldn't give him.

Dear Future Grandchildren,

You will inherit a world where love comes in more forms than your ancestors could imagine. Where families are chosen as much as they're born. Where authenticity matters more than approval. I pray you'll know that kind of freedom from the beginning, so you never have to spend decades finding your way back to yourself.

I love you all from this distance. I'm proud of who you're becoming, even though I'll never get to see it up close.

WHAT I WOULD TELL OTHER PARENTS

If you're reading this and you recognize yourself in these words, if you're the mother whose child won't speak to you since you left their father, if you're the father whose son can't forgive your bankruptcy, your addiction, your mental health struggles, your truth, know this:

Their rejection of you doesn't negate the love you gave them. The bedtime stories still happened. The soccer practices still mattered. The way you showed up when they were sick, scared, or celebrating, none of that becomes retroactively meaningless because they're angry now.

You are allowed to grieve this loss. Even if others think you "brought it on yourself." Even if the choice was ultimately yours. Even if you would make the same choice again. Loss is loss, and missing your child is one of the purest forms of heartbreak that exists.

Your truth was not a betrayal of them. Living authentically whether that's about sexuality, spirituality, mental health, life choices, or any other fundamental part of who you are, is not an act of selfishness. Continuing to lie would have been a different kind of harm.

They may come back. Not today, maybe not for years, but love has a way of surviving even the deepest rifts. Hold space for that possibility without depending on it. Heal without requiring their participation in your healing.

You can still be proud of who they become. From a distance, with no credit, you can still celebrate their achievements, worry about their struggles, and hope for their happiness. That's what love looks like sometimes caring without being able to express it.

THE LONG VIEW

I've been writing unsent letters for three years now. Some are angry. Some are desperate. Some are achingly tender. All of them are honest in ways I couldn't be when it mattered most.

Maybe someday I'll send one. Maybe they'll find these words after I'm gone and understand something they couldn't when I was here to explain. Maybe their own children will ask questions that lead them back to the truth about who I was and why I made the choices I made.

Or maybe this silence will be permanent, and these letters will remain the only place where I get to be their father.

Either way, I keep writing. Because love doesn't stop just because it can't be expressed. Because somewhere in the act of putting words on paper, I'm still parenting—still trying to give them something of value, even if they'll never receive it.

The hardest lesson of parenthood isn't how to protect your children from the world. It's how to love them when they need to protect themselves from you.

I'm still learning. I'll probably be learning for the rest of my life.

But I'm still here. Still their father. Still proud. Still sorry. Still hoping that love, somehow, finds a way.

If you're estranged from your child for whatever reason, whatever choices led to this silence… you're not alone. The love doesn't disappear just because they do. Write the letters. Feel the feelings. Grieve the relationship while holding space for the possibility that love, in some form, might find its way back to you both.

And remember you are still a parent, even in the silence. That part of your identity doesn't require their permission to exist

CHAPTER 8

THE GEOGRAPHY OF HEALING

FINDING SACRED GROUND

Florida became more than a location it became a laboratory for learning how to live authentically. Here, among palm trees and rainbow crosswalks, I began the slow work of integration. Not just accepting that I was gay but figuring out what that meant in the context of everything else I was: father, friend, professional, human being trying to make sense of a complicated world.

This concept of geographical healing isn't unique to my story. We all need spaces where we can practice being ourselves where the rules that constrained us elsewhere don't apply. For some, it's a college campus hundreds of miles from home. For others, it's an art studio, a support group, a hiking trail, or even just a coffee shop where nobody knows their history.

Psychologists call these "identity-congruent environments" they are spaces where who you are and how you're expected to behave align naturally. Research shows that people experiencing major identity transitions need these environments to practice new ways of being before integrating them into their broader lives.

Wilton Manors offered community, but it wasn't the community I had imagined. These weren't people who wanted to rescue me from my past or fix me for my future. They were simply people living their lives openly, creating space for others to do the same.

I learned to exist without constantly calculating the cost of visibility. To laugh without wondering if it sounded right. To express affection without fear of judgment. These sound like small things, but they felt revolutionary like learning to walk after years of crawling.

THE PSYCHOLOGY OF SAFE SPACES

What I discovered in Florida mirrors what therapists call "psychological safety" the belief that you can be yourself without risk of punishment or humiliation. Dr. Amy Edmondson's research shows that psychological safety is crucial not just for workplace performance, but for personal growth and authentic self-expression.

In psychologically safe environments, we:

- Take risks without fear of retribution
- Express ourselves without excessive self-monitoring
- Learn from mistakes instead of hiding them
- Ask for help without feeling weak
- Show emotion without shame

For anyone navigating major life transitions, whether related to sexuality, career changes, recovery from addiction, leaving abusive relationships, or any other fundamental shift, finding these environments is essential. They serve as training grounds for authenticity.

Creating Your Own Safe Spaces:

If geographical change isn't possible, you can cultivate psychological safety in smaller ways:

- **Online communities** where anonymity allows for honest exploration
- **Therapeutic relationships** that provide unconditional acceptance
- **Support groups** with shared experiences
- **Creative outlets** where self-expression is encouraged
- **Spiritual communities** that embrace rather than judge
- **Physical activities** where your body can exist without performance pressure

The key is finding spaces where you can practice being yourself in low-stakes environments before facing higher-stakes situations.

Building New Traditions:
The Architecture of Belonging

Holidays were the hardest to navigate. Christmas morning without children's voices, Thanksgiving without a table full of biological family, birthdays celebrated quietly or not at all. I had to learn to create meaning in solitude, to build traditions that didn't rely on people who were no longer part of my story.

This challenge of rebuilding rituals and traditions faces anyone whose life has been fundamentally disrupted. The divorced person spending their first holiday alone. The person in recovery avoiding family gatherings centered around alcohol. The individual who left their religious community and lost the rhythm of weekly services and annual celebrations.

But I also discovered the profound healing power of chosen traditions. Friends who became chosen family. Communities that gather around shared experience rather than shared DNA. Love that isn't contingent on performance or conditional on conformity.

THE PSYCHOLOGY OF RITUAL AND BELONGING:

Anthropologist Arnold van Gennep identified three stages in all meaningful transitions: separation, liminality, and reintegration. Most of us get stuck in the middle phase, the liminal space where we've left the old but haven't yet fully entered the new.

Creating new traditions helps us move from liminality to reintegration by:

- **Providing structure** when old frameworks have collapsed
- **Creating meaning** around new identities and relationships
- **Building community** with people who accept our authentic selves

- **Establishing continuity** between our past and future selves
- **Offering predictability** in the midst of major change

PRACTICAL STEPS FOR BUILDING NEW TRADITIONS:

1. **Start Small:** A weekly coffee with a supportive friend can become as meaningful as any family dinner
2. **Honor Your Values:** Create rituals around what matters to you now, not what you think should matter
3. **Include Others:** Invite people who are also building new traditions, you can create community together
4. **Allow Evolution:** Traditions don't have to be permanent; they can change as you grow
5. **Blend Old and New:** Keep meaningful elements from your past while adding new components

The family I built in Florida looked nothing like the family I had been born into or the family I had created through marriage. But it was family nonetheless, people who showed up when life got difficult, who celebrated successes without reservation, who loved without asterisks.

THE NEUROSCIENCE OF SELF-COMPASSION

Learning to forgive myself was harder than forgiving anyone else. The voice in my head that catalogued every mistake, every moment of cowardice, every choice that hurt someone I loved that voice was louder and more persistent than any external criticism.

This internal critic is what psychologists call our "inner hostile voice" the internalized version of all the criticism, shame, and rejection we've experienced throughout our lives. Neuroscience research shows that this voice activates the same threat-detection systems in our brain as external danger, flooding our bodies with stress hormones.

Dr. Kristin Neff's groundbreaking research on self-compassion reveals that treating ourselves with kindness isn't just nice, it's neurologically necessary for healing and growth. Self-compassion involves three components:

1. **Self-Kindness**: Treating yourself with the same gentleness you'd offer a good friend
2. **Common Humanity**: Recognizing that struggle and imperfection are part of the shared human experience
3. **Mindful Awareness**: Observing your thoughts and feelings without getting overwhelmed by them

THE COMPLEX WORK OF INTEGRATION

I had to learn to hold complexity without demanding resolution. To accept that I could simultaneously be proud of my courage in claiming my truth and devastated by the cost that courage required. To understand that growth doesn't erase the past, it just changes how we carry it.

This capacity to hold paradox, what psychologists call "dialectical thinking" is crucial for mental health and authentic living. It means accepting that:

- You can love someone and still need to set boundaries with them
- You can be grateful for your past while being glad it's over
- You can be proud of your growth while grieving what you lost
- You can be angry at someone's choices while having compassion for their struggles
- You can celebrate your authenticity while mourning the relationships it cost

PRACTICAL EXERCISES FOR DEVELOPING DIALECTICAL THINKING:

1. **"Both/And" Practice**: When you catch yourself in black-and-white thinking, practice saying "both" instead of "but"
2. **Emotion Validation**: Notice multiple feelings can coexist—you can be nervous AND excited, sad AND relieved
3. **Perspective Taking**: Practice seeing situations from multiple angles without needing to choose one as "right"
4. **Temporal Integration**: Remember that who you were, who you are, and who you're becoming can all coexist

Therapy helped, but ultimately forgiveness was a daily practice, a choice I had to make again and again. Some days it felt genuine. Other days it felt like one more performance. But even performed forgiveness, I learned, is better than its absence.

THE RIPPLE EFFECTS OF AUTHENTICITY

What I discovered in my geographical healing journey was that authenticity is contagious. When we show up as ourselves, messy, complex, real, we give others permission to do the same. The courage to be vulnerable creates spaces where others can be vulnerable too.

Research by Dr. Brené Brown confirms that vulnerability is not weakness but the birthplace of courage, creativity, and change. When we stop performing and start being, we model a different way of existing in the world.

This has implications beyond personal healing:

- **In families**: One person's authenticity can break generational patterns of hiding and shame
- **In workplaces**: Psychological safety created by one person's openness can transform entire team dynamics
- **In communities**: Visible authenticity challenges others to examine their own masks
- **In relationships**: Genuine connection becomes possible when performance ends

CREATING YOUR OWN GEOGRAPHY OF HEALING

Whether or not you can physically relocate, you can create spaces for authentic living:

Environmental Design:

- Arrange your living space to reflect your true self, not others' expectations
- Create a private sanctuary where you can be completely yourself
- Display art, books, or objects that represent your authentic identity

Social Architecture:

- Gradually spend more time with people who accept your authentic self
- Practice small acts of authenticity in low-risk situations
- Joining communities built around shared interests rather than shared performances

Psychological Landscape:

- Develop mindfulness practices that help you notice when you're performing versus being
- Challenge the internal voices that demand conformity
- Cultivate self-compassion as the foundation for all other healing

Temporal Healing:

- Create new traditions that reflect your current values and relationships
- Establish regular practices that honor your authentic self
- Build routines that support rather than suppress your true nature

THE LONG ARC OF INTEGRATION

Healing geography isn't just about finding a place where you can be yourself, it's about becoming someone who can be authentic anywhere. The external safe spaces teach us what internal safety feels like, so we can eventually carry that safety with us.

The goal isn't to stay forever in the healing place, but to learn from it how to transform other spaces. To bring the authenticity you practiced in safe environments into the more challenging arenas of your life.

Some days you'll succeed. Some days you'll slip back into performance mode. Both are part of the journey. The geography of healing isn't a destination, it's a map for learning to be at home in your own skin, wherever that skin happens to be.

And once you learn that geography, once you know the way home to yourself, you can help others find their own paths to authenticity. Because healing, like authenticity, is contagious. And the world needs more people who know the way.

CHAPTER 9

THE SILENCE AFTER THE COLLAPSE

THE MOMENT OF FRACTURE

Right after the truth escapes your lips, time doesn't progress it compresses. The world doesn't explode. No one shouts. Nothing shatters visibly. But inside, something fundamental shifts. It's quiet, almost imperceptible, yet it reverberates through your entire being like a tuning fork struck in silence.

Your body registers the rupture before your mind can name it. Shoulders tighten instinctively. Breath becomes hesitant, measured. The pulse stumbles, missing beats. It's like standing motionless on the edge of a cliff while the earth beneath you begins to fracture not dramatically, but with the slow, inevitable certainty of geological time.

That was the moment I began to collapse not in a dramatic outward spiral that others could witness and respond to, but in a slow, internal unraveling that would take months to fully understand. Psychologists call this emotional dissonance: when your internal reality no longer matches the external world you're expected to navigate. The nervous system responds before cognition catches up, a survival mechanism rooted deep in the brain's limbic system, ancient as fear itself.

In that moment, my body wasn't betraying me, it was protecting me from a truth too large to process all at once.

THE GEOGRAPHY OF GRIEF

Three weeks after the collapse

Grief didn't arrive like the storm I expected. It crept in like condensation on windows, silent, persistent, until it had saturated everything I touched. The first place I felt it wasn't my heart, as poets promised it would be. It was my spine. A dull, unyielding pressure that nestled between my shoulder blades like a stone I couldn't dislodge, whispering accusations I couldn't silence: *You've disappointed everyone who ever loved you.*

It wasn't spoken aloud, but it brushed against me like a chill I couldn't shake, no matter how many layers I added.

My body became a reluctant archive of the collapse, storing what my mind couldn't yet process. Breathing grew shallow not from exertion, but from emotional restraint. I feared that a full breath might unlock the floodgates of feeling I wasn't ready to face. My posture curled inward, instinctively shielding a heart too tender to remain exposed to the world.

Sleep offered no sanctuary from this new geography of pain. Nights turned into battlegrounds—sweat-soaked sheets, clenched fists, a jaw aching from grinding guilt into silence. I'd wake before dawn and sit on the edge of the bed, staring at floorboards that seemed to groan under the weight of everything unsaid, everything that could never be unsaid.

Even the simple act of dressing became a ritual of disconnection. I chose clothes like I was outfitting someone else for a role I no longer understood. I looked in the mirror not to assess my appearance, but to confirm my existence. What stared back was a version of me that was present but fragmented moving through space but never quite arriving anywhere.

This was somatic grief in its purest form, where emotional pain manifests as physical reality. Trauma researchers have documented how the body stores unresolved emotions in muscle tension, disrupted sleep patterns, and chronic fatigue that no amount of rest can cure. Grief doesn't just live in the mind it settles into tissue and bone, becoming part of our physical architecture. And healing, I would learn, begins when we stop fighting these sensations and start listening to what they're trying to tell us.

THE PERFORMANCE OF NORMAL

Two months into the collapse

But this internal revolution had to coexist with the external world's expectation of continuity. On the surface, I remained unchanged. I smiled in meetings with the same practiced warmth. Replied to texts with appropriate enthusiasm. Wore the same professional uniforms. Locked the same doors each night with the same careful ritual.

The gap between these two realities, inner collapse and outer competence, created a strange kind of vertigo.

Inside, my emotional infrastructure was crumbling like a building whose foundation had shifted. I was living in two bodies: one that the world could see composed, articulate, steady and another that existed behind my ribs, where anxiety pressed down like a weight I couldn't lift, couldn't name, couldn't explain to anyone who asked if I was okay.

Navigating daily life felt like watching a stranger reenact my routines with mechanical precision. I poured coffee with hands that seemed borrowed. Sent emails in a voice that sounded like mine but felt hollow. Said things like "I'm fine" and "Just tired" with the conviction of someone who had practiced these lines until they felt almost true.

But I wasn't inhabiting my life, I was impersonating it. Mimicking a version of myself who hadn't yet unraveled, who still believed in the story, we'd all agreed to tell about who I was and what I wanted.

This wasn't grief that followed the predictable arc I'd read about in psychology textbooks. It was chaotic, non-linear a haunting that clung to my skin like smoke from a fire I couldn't locate. I tried to mask it with structured sentences and practiced smiles, but my body betrayed me at every turn: twitching eyelids, mysterious aches, a fatigue that sleep couldn't touch. It was a silent rebellion against the illusion I was working so hard to maintain.

What I was experiencing, I would later learn, psychologists call functional dissociation a sophisticated coping mechanism where we maintain outward normalcy while becoming emotionally disconnected from our own experience. It's particularly common among high-functioning individuals navigating trauma, those of us who have learned that the show must go on regardless of what's happening backstage.

But survival, I was beginning to understand, isn't the same as healing. And pretending to be okay is not the same as being okay.

THE LETTER I COULDN'T FINISH

Four months after the collapse

There was a letter I started writing during this period dozens of versions, actually, all beginning with the same line: "I'm afraid that grief hasn't just broken my heart. I think it's rewired it."

I could never get past that opening. Every time I tried to continue, the words felt inadequate, too small for what I was trying to describe. How do you explain that you're mourning not just what you've lost, but who you used to be? How do you tell someone that you're grieving your own previous certainties, the version of yourself that used to know how to move through the world?

I'm afraid that grief hasn't just broken my heart. I think it's rewired it. Nothing feels the same anymore. Coffee tastes different. Colors look muted. Even kindness feels suspicious, like something

I don't deserve or don't know how to receive. I recoil from gentle touches not because they hurt, but because they remind me I'm still capable of feeling, and feeling seems dangerous right now.

I used to think healing meant going back to who I was before. But what if there is no before anymore? What if this is just who I am now, someone who has seen behind the curtain of his own life and can never pretend he doesn't know what's back there?

I'm not writing this for answers. I'm writing because the silence inside my head has become too loud, and I need to put these words somewhere outside of myself, even if no one ever reads them.

That line "I think it's rewired it" lingered in my mind for weeks. It explained why I recoiled from kindness, why simple gestures of care felt like dragging stones uphill. My body moved with the memory of old habits, but my spirit moved with the caution of something that had learned that the world wasn't as safe as it once seemed.

Nothing was visibly wrong with my life, yet nothing felt right. It was like living in a house where all the furniture had been moved slightly everything familiar, but nothing quite where you expected it to be.

THE SHIFT TOWARD INTEGRATION

Six months after the collapse

In those quiet, unobserved moments usually in the early morning when the world was still soft with possibility a whisper of clarity began to emerge: I wasn't weak, I was wounded. I wasn't failing, I was feeling. Feeling the full weight of having loved deeply and lost something irreplaceable.

That distinction felt revolutionary.

Grief, I began to understand, wasn't a flaw in my emotional system, it was a testament to it. The deeper the ache, the deeper the bond that preceded it. Neuroscience research confirms this: emotional trauma doesn't just hurt us, it literally reshapes our neural pathways. The heart doesn't just break, it recalibrates. And in that recalibration, we begin to understand that healing isn't about returning to some previous baseline.

It's about creating a new one.

This shift from survival mode to integration happened gradually, almost imperceptibly. I started to notice moments when I wasn't just enduring my days but actually inhabiting them. A laugh that felt genuine rather than performed. A conversation where I wasn't constantly monitoring how I appeared to others. A morning when I woke up curious about what might happen rather than dreading what I'd have to get through.

When we begin to reclaim our authentic voice not the one, we use to shield others from our reality, but the one that speaks our actual experience we move from being defined by our pain to being informed by it. Expression, whether through words, movement, or art, becomes not just catharsis but reclamation of our right to exist as we actually are.

WHAT SURVIVES THE COLLAPSE

Eight months later

And yet, in that fractured silence where everything felt uncertain, something unexpected stirred. Faint at first, like the whisper of circulation returning to a limb that had been numb. A flicker of sensation in the soles of my feet. A breath that reached slightly deeper than the ones before it.

I didn't call it hope, not yet. That word felt too bold for what I was experiencing. But it felt like the beginning of something stubbornly unwilling to die.

Grief had once been the loudest voice in the room, drowning out everything else with its insistent narrative of loss and regret. But now, another voice was emerging my own. Not the voice I'd used for decades to comfort others and maintain appearances, but the one I was learning to use for myself. Raw, uncertain, but undeniably real.

With that voice came a strange kind of peace. Not the kind that erases pain or pretends difficulty doesn't exist, but the kind that names what is actually happening. That transforms suffering from a monster lurking in the shadows into a map of where you've been and where you might go next.

This is what integration actually looks like not the dramatic breakthrough moments we see in movies, but the quiet daily practice of telling ourselves the truth about our experience and learning to trust that we can handle that truth.

THE ARCHITECTURE OF HEALING

One year after the collapse

Healing, I was learning, doesn't mean returning to who you were before the earthquake. It means becoming someone new, shaped, not shattered, by what you've endured. It's not about forgetting the fracture or fixing what broke. It's about facing the fault lines honestly and choosing to grow around them, through them, because of them.

This understanding became my turning point. Not triumphant in the way I might have once imagined. Not tidy or complete. But true in a way that felt sustainable.

The man who emerged from this collapse wasn't the same person who had entered it. He was more tender in some ways, more resilient in others. He had learned the difference between being broken and being broken open. He understood that some kinds of falling apart are actually a form of coming together with reality, with authenticity, with the person you were always meant to be but were too afraid to become.

So, I end this chapter not with resolution because healing isn't a destination but a practice but with recognition. Recognition of the man who bent but didn't break. Who hurt but still reached for softness when it was offered. Who lost his footing but never abandoned the path toward becoming more fully himself.

Because even in the deepest silence, even when everything felt uncertain, I was still moving. And in that movement, I began to remember not who I was before the collapse, but who I was becoming because of it.

Healing is architectural. We don't rebuild the same structure that fell we design something new with the materials left behind. We use the rubble to create stronger foundations, wider windows, doors that open more easily. And in that design, we find not just recovery, but rebirth. Not just survival, but a life worth surviving for.

The collapse, I finally understood, wasn't the end of my story. It was the demolition that made space for something better to be built

CHAPTER 10

THE BODY REMEMBERS

There's a moment, right after the truth leaves your mouth, when your body braces like an animal sensing an unseen predator. The skin tightens. The breath holds. The heartbeat stumbles. Even though no explosion erupts around you, something inside begins to fracture your nervous system flooding with signals meant for physical danger, though the threat exists only in the space between what was said and what cannot be unsaid.

This is the body's ancient wisdom at work. It doesn't wait for logic. It doesn't ask for permission. It simply reacts. And in that reaction, it teaches us something vital: when your body speaks, listen. It knows what your mind hasn't yet admitted.

THE INVASION

Grief didn't arrive like a thunderstorm. It seeped slowly, a silent flood that rose with every breath I took. My spine felt it first not as pain, but as pressure. A weight between my shoulder blades that whispered You've disappointed them with every step I tried to take.

I walked differently after the collapse. My shoulders didn't just hunch; they collapsed inward, unconsciously shielding a heart too bruised for exposure. My posture became a fortress, protecting me from judgment that existed mostly in my own mind.

My breath shortened not from exertion, but from constraint. It was as if grief had wrapped itself around my lungs, squeezing gently until oxygen became a negotiation. Even in safety, my body refused to trust it.

And here's what I learned: grief doesn't just live in your thoughts, it settles into your bones, your breath, your stance. Healing begins not with fixing the mind, but with honoring the body's silent protest.

THE BATTLEGROUND

Sleep offered no refuge. I'd lie down and feel the cool sheets against my skin, but comfort never reached the core. Without daylight's distractions, nighttime amplified every internal alarm. Dreams came disjointed and loud. I'd wake at 2 AM drenched in sweat despite the cold house, my pillow bearing imprints of clenched fists, my jaw aching from grinding down guilt through the night.

Some mornings, my limbs felt heavy, as if grief had moved in and filled my bones with cement. I'd sit on the edge of my bed, staring at floorboards that seemed to groan under the weight of what was lost.

Even the smallest gestures became strange rituals. Stirring coffee. Choosing clothes. Locking the door. Each action felt disconnected from meaning, like I was imitating the life I used to know.

This was survival in disguise. A kind of emotional dissociation that mimicked routine but lacked presence. And yet, even imitation is a form of endurance. When meaning disappears, ritual holds the line until it returns.

THE ARCHIVE

When I caught my reflection in the mirror, I wasn't looking for sorrow I was confronting absence. A hollowing. The person staring back felt like a stranger wearing my face, present but not whole, moving but not truly arriving anywhere.

Grief wasn't a shadow I could outrun; it had become a second skin. It followed me into meetings, meals, conversations. When I tried to mask it with practiced smiles or rigid structure, my body betrayed me with small rebellions, a twitch, a tremor, a breath caught mid-sentence.

My body had become a living archive of the collapse, carrying not just the memory of what happened, but the blueprint of how I'd learned to survive it.

And in that realization, I found a truth: your body is not your enemy it's your witness. It remembers what you've endured, and it holds the map to where you've been. To heal, you must stop fighting it and start reading it.

THE STIRRING

And yet, even in that haunted frame, something stirred. A pulse that refused to die. A tremor of defiance in the soles of my feet. A quiet breath that finally reached the bottom of my lungs.

It wasn't dramatic, not a roar, but a whisper. The smallest shift. What psychologists call *post-traumatic growth*: a gentle rebuilding that takes shape beneath the rubble. Not healing in its final form, but the first signs of life returning after devastation.

My psyche, exhausted and fractured, was slowly tracing the outline of hope again.

And I understood: healing doesn't announce itself. It arrives quietly, disguised as breath, as movement, as the decision to try again. Pay attention to the whispers, they are the beginning of your return.

THE PERMISSION

Grief had scorched me. But in the ash, I found something unexpected: I was still here. Not whole. Not healed. But awake.

So, I moved. Not with confidence or certainty, but with the quiet permission to exist.

It started with the mirror. A tilt of my head not to admire, but to acknowledge. The reflection didn't offer comfort, just presence. I stood there, still fractured, still reassembling, and allowed myself to be seen.

Then came the slightest shift. My shoulders once armor, once refuge eased downward. Not lifted in triumph, just no longer curled in defense. A breath. A step. Then another.

It wasn't bold. It wasn't brave. But it was real.

And that was enough. You don't need to be whole to be worthy. You don't need to be healed to be seen. You only need to give yourself permission to exist as you are.

THE LANGUAGE OF RECOVERY

This was the moment when survival stopped being mere reaction and began to look like intention. When my body and mind, after seasons of discord, began to speak the same language again. A quiet unison. A slow emergence. The early architecture of healing.

It wasn't redemption. But it was a new start.

My body, this living archive of collapse, had remembered the weight of loss. Now it was learning the rhythm of release. The silence after the collapse wasn't empty anymore, it carried echoes of what I'd survived and who I was becoming.

For the first time in months, I didn't flinch from those echoes.

I listened.

And in that listening, I learned: recovery isn't a finish line, it's a conversation. Between body and mind. Between past and present. Between who you were and who you're becoming. Speak gently. Listen deeply. That's how healing begins.

CHAPTER 11

LIVING AS ME

I t didn't happen overnight. There was no sunrise epiphany, no dramatic transformation, no swelling music or cinematic closure. Just small, aching steps toward something I'd never truly known myself.

And that's the first truth of becoming it's not a moment, it's a movement. One that begins quietly, often in the absence of applause. The journey inward rarely announces itself. It arrives in fragments, in pauses, in the soft refusal to keep pretending.

WINTER'S END

Healing began not with a triumphant cry but with a breath held beneath blankets in what felt like perpetual winter. My bed, once a battlefield of sleepless nights and clenched jaws, slowly became a sanctuary. I curled into it not as a fugitive anymore, but as someone relearning rest.

Each morning, the floor chilled my bare feet a reminder that I was still alive, still moving. I'd light candles not for ambiance but to mark time: *You are here. You are whole. You are allowed to begin again.*

The rituals were simple: morning walks without checking my phone, reading books without pretending to be someone else in the margins, learning to sit in silence without fearing it might echo back the pieces I'd lost.

At first, it felt like living in ruins. I had burned bridges I once believed were indestructible. I had hurt people I loved. And yet, for the first time in my life, I was no longer disappearing into the shape of someone else's expectations.

Rest is not laziness, it's resistance. In a world that demands performance, choosing stillness is a radical act of self-respect. I wasn't escaping anymore. I was arriving.

THE RISK OF BLOOM

Spring arrived quietly on the edges of my breath, with breezes that smelled like forgiveness. In the early morning hours, I walked beneath trees dusted in white petals, uncertain whether growth was happening inside me too. The light in the kitchen felt gentler. The walls, which had once felt tight with grief, now breathed with possibility.

I began to stretch nothing dramatic, just morning movement. My shoulders unfurled like frostbitten vines testing warmth. I no longer braced myself in rooms full of performances I had spent years perfecting. I stood without armor.

Change arrived uneasy and confusing. It was as if overnight, the life I had learned to live vanished, and in its place, emerged a landscape I didn't recognize.

Growth rarely feels graceful. It feels awkward, uncertain, and exposed. But that discomfort is proof you're no longer shrinking to fit a life that wasn't yours. I wasn't blooming for anyone else. I was blooming for me.

SUMMER'S QUESTIONS

Light poured through windows and across floors I once paced with doubt. I sat longer in that light now. The air was heavier, full of scents I had forgotten how to welcome: cut grass, pavement heat, lavender drifting through an open window.

I walked to the beach alone, simply to think and try to discover who I genuinely was. The salt water didn't cleanse me it met me. I floated face to sky and felt my grief loosen beneath me. It wasn't gone, but it was lighter.

During this season of reflection, people who once called or texted regularly faded into silence. I questioned everything again. Had I made a mistake? Should I have remained in my make-believe world, allowing the shadow of my true self to stay buried? Was authenticity worth this loneliness?

Living as me meant asking hard questions: What do I want now that I'm no longer performing? What does love look like when it's not tied to guilt? What does success mean when no one's watching?

Loneliness is not always a sign of failure. Sometimes it's the space required for truth to grow. When you stop performing, not everyone stays but what remains is real. And real, I was learning, is enough.

Autumn's Release

Like leaves falling to the ground, elements of my past began to drop away. I cleared old closets. Deleted old messages. Made soup slowly. My kitchen, once filled with the noise of performance, became a haven for aroma and pause. Cinnamon, cardamom, rosemary each scent stitched warmth into my body's cold edges.

It was during this time I understood: The price of living an authentic life is high. But it's the only currency I've ever truly owned.

This became a time of personal reflection in the shadow of silence new territory, unmapped, with no guide or manual. Only the quiet beating of a heart learning its own rhythm.

Letting go is not forgetting. It's choosing what deserves space in your present. Release is not weakness, it's wisdom. And wisdom, I found, often speaks in whispers.

The Choice

Excitement flickered, balanced by moments of raw, unshakable fear. Loss stood like a monument to what once was. But just beyond it, possibility whispered.

I could mourn the make-believe, grieve the fading echoes of who I thought I had to be. Or I could reach forward, not knowing what might take shape but certain that movement itself was a form of hope.

In the silence of my existence, I made my choice: to press on.

You don't need clarity to move forward. You only need courage. Choosing yourself is not selfish, it's sacred. And sacred things are often quiet.

What Remains

Living as me isn't about proving anything anymore. It's about peace not the loud, victorious kind, but the kind that slips in at dusk and curls beside you like breath.

Some days still hurt. Some memories still sting. But they no longer define me.

What defines me now is the truth I no longer run from the slow, steady rhythm of a life lived without masks, without apology, without the exhausting performance of being anyone other than exactly who I am.

And that, I'm learning, is enough.

Enoughness isn't earned. It's remembered. You were never meant to be anyone else. The most radical thing you can do is live as yourself and let that be enough

CHAPTER 12

BRICK BY BRICK

There's no blueprint for rebuilding your life after it's fallen apart. No map for the aftermath of becoming. Just rubble, memory, and the quiet ache of possibility.

Psychologists call this phase identity reconstruction, the slow, uncertain process of piecing together a self that's no longer defined by roles, expectations, or illusions. It's not about returning to who you were. It's about discovering who you are when everything else is stripped away.

SURVIVAL

In the beginning, rebuilding looked like survival. Waking up when I didn't want to. Making coffee for one. Learning how to fill an empty Saturday without guilt or noise.

I had to teach myself how to live without the roles that once defined me no longer the picture-perfect husband, no longer the charming professional, no longer anyone's safe illusion. Just me, raw and undefined, trying to figure out what that even meant.

Survival is not weakness it's wisdom. It's the body and mind doing what they must to keep going, even when the soul hasn't caught up. In trauma recovery, this is known as adaptive functioning the ability to maintain life's basics while the deeper healing waits its turn.

And so, I survived. Not gracefully. Not heroically. But honestly.

THE QUESTIONS

Slowly, survival gave way to something deeper: inquiry. I started asking the questions I'd long avoided: *Who am I without lies? Who am I without the need to be palatable, without the armor of performance?*

I tried on truths like thrift-store jackets. Some fit. Some didn't. But I gave myself permission to be fluid, to be uncertain, to feel instead of performing. Each question was both terrifying and liberating a small death of who I thought I had to be, and a small birth of who I might become.

This is the heart of self-concept exploration a psychological process where we dismantle inherited identities and begin to author our own. It's messy. It's nonlinear. But it's necessary.

Growth doesn't come from answers it comes from asking better questions.

THE STORM

Then came the consequences. A tornado of my own making that tore through everything I knew, leaving a landscape barren and bewildering. Nothing familiar remained, yet everything felt strangely inevitable. It made no sense, but it made all the sense in the world.

I found myself without family, without friends, in a city that no longer felt like mine. The isolation was crushing, but it was also clarifying. When everything external falls away, what remains is either nothing or everything that actually matters.

This is what psychologists call existential crisis a confrontation with meaning, identity, and mortality. It's not a breakdown. It's a breakthrough.

Sometimes the storm isn't punishment it's permission. To rebuild. To reimagine. To begin again.

The Move

The transition had started long before the collapse a quiet beginning, buying a small business in Florida, commuting back and forth, unintentionally shedding layers I didn't know were suffocating me. Authenticity, it seems, has a way of breaking open the new, especially when we cling hardest to illusion.

So, I moved to Florida full-time and began again. Afraid, but moving. Uncertain, but present. A soul in reconstruction, finally building a life of my own making.

Change doesn't wait for readiness. It arrives when truth becomes louder than fear. And when it does, the only way forward is through.

THE COST

Truth meant owning the harm I'd caused, especially to my boys who meant the world to me. It required accepting that the damage might mean a life without them, or without the friends I once knew and loved. Trust is fragile currency hard to earn, harder still when you've shattered it.

The fear of isolation was real. Some nights, I wondered if authenticity was worth this loneliness, if living truthfully was worth losing everything I thought I couldn't live without.

But the alternative returning to the suffocating performance of a life that was never really mine felt like a different kind of death.

This is the paradox of moral injury, the psychological pain of knowing you've violated your own values or hurt others in the process of becoming yourself.

Healing requires accountability. Not to erase the past, but to honor it with honesty.

REDISCOVERING

Gradually, through the debris of what was lost, I began to rediscover not just who I was, but what I loved. Music that made my chest ache in the best way. Places that felt like belonging. Conversations that didn't need footnotes or edits. People who met me in the middle not to save me, but to walk with me.

I was a jigsaw of thought and emotion, struggling to separate fiction from fact, memory from mythology. But this journey, as disjointed and unsure as it felt, was the only way forward.

Rediscovery is not about finding what was, it's about noticing what's still alive. In trauma therapy, this is called reconnection the slow return to joy, meaning, and relationship.

THE BLOOMING

It wasn't a grand rebirth. It was a slow blooming moment here, a small victory there. A day when I laughed without guilt. A night when I didn't second-guess the person staring back at me in the mirror.

I didn't become someone new. I came home to someone I'd buried long ago under layers of expectation, performance, and fear.

The man who emerged wasn't perfect or fully healed. He was real. Flawed. Honest. And for the first time in my life, he was enough.

AT LAST

This uneven, humbling, sacred journey isn't over. It never is. But now I walk it with open hands, no longer grasping for approval or hiding from judgment.

No more performing. No more shrinking.

Just me.

At last.

And that's the final lesson: healing isn't a destination, it's a devotion. To truth. To self. To the life you're finally brave enough to live.

CHAPTER 13

LOVING THE GHOSTS
THAT STAY BEHIND

A SKY OF UNSPOKEN GOODBYES

Some goodbyes don't echo with sound, but with absence, like stars still glowing in the sky long after death. These weren't goodbyes shouted in doorways or sealed with slammed phones. They happened in sighs too quiet to hear. In pauses that stretched like empty constellations, swallowing whole conversations. In the shift from warm light to an empty chair across the table.

Psychologists call this kind of loss "ambiguous grief." There are no casseroles for the fading of a friendship. No funerals when a parent forgets how to dial your number. But the ache is real and often more disorienting than death. Because it's not the end that hurts most, it's how the silence wraps itself around your memories, until even the laughter feels like it happened in a different universe.

Coming out didn't just mean change; it meant cost. It meant watching stars fall from my own galaxy. Once drawn to me like planets to the sun, my children now float in a different orbit. My friends, who once knew my favorite coffee and the rhythm of my laugh, suddenly spoke in tones that felt distant and brittle, as if my truth broke the telescope they'd used to see me.

They never knew about the nights I felt like a stranger in my own skin. Or the dreams I'd buried so deep I almost forgot I had them. Something shifted between me and them when I finally dared to name my truth in us. The constellation we had built together is gone.

Authenticity is a strange kind of star. It glows from the inside, illuminating your soul. But sometimes that same light blinds others who've only known your shadows. Research says it's vital for self-esteem, for resilience, for joy. But the research doesn't prepare you for the cold that follows. The frost that gathers around people you once loved fiercely.

There was no shouting. No drama. Just a quiet turning away. A polite distance wrapped in smiles and small talk. They didn't stop speaking; they stopped *seeing*. And my body, wiser than I knew, flinched like it had been struck because social rejection lights up the same parts of the brain as physical pain. And this? This was a slow, freezing ache.

They loved the version of me that fit neatly in their story. But not the messy, glowing truth I finally let rise like the moon. And there's a unique kind of heartbreak in realizing someone can love you deeply, but only conditionally if you dim only if you orbit *them*.

Real intimacy needs more. It needs radical acceptance, the kind that doesn't demand you shrink. Without that, love becomes performance. Transaction. Cage.

But even in this grief, there's clarity, a knowing. I no longer want to be loved in fragments. I no longer want to be seen through someone else's cracked lens.

So, I stand beneath the sky of what was and ask myself not with bitterness, but with quiet hope. *What kind of love do I want to build my life around?*

UNDER THE SAME STARRY SKY

The world kept spinning, polite and polished, like nothing had changed. But something had. The light that once shimmered behind familiar faces had dimmed. Their kindness remained, but it came wrapped in distance, like the moon behind a fogged window, still present but unreachable.

I noticed it in the smallest gestures: the way they avoided lingering too long in my presence, the shift in how they asked about my life, no longer curious, just cordial. Like they were checking a box, they hadn't slammed the door; they'd left it ajar and walked away slowly enough that I couldn't quite call it abandonment.

Maybe that's what made it harder.

One evening, I sat at the window, watching the sky unravel above me in velvet blue and bruised purple shades. The stars blinked, soft and stubborn, refusing to disappear. I imagined the world as Van Gogh must have seen it, swirled with feeling, thick with loneliness, beautiful in a way that others might mistake for madness. I thought, *maybe that's me now. A painting only, I can understand.*

I remembered something I'd read once: *Social rejection activates the same parts of the brain as physical pain.* I believed it. My chest ached in ways I couldn't name. The hurt wasn't sharp like heartbreak; it was dull and haunting, a slow erosion. The warmth between us had drained like water from a cracked cup.

It wasn't anger that consumed me. It was the absence of recognition. The subtle disappearance of being known.

I used to soften my truth. I thought if I made it palatable, more people would stay. But no matter how gentle I made my story, it still made some flinch. And I realized, *"I don't know how to love you now,"* wasn't something they'd say aloud. It was something their silence whispered.

And yet, I couldn't bring myself to hate them.

There's a certain kind of grief that doesn't ask for funerals. The kind that comes when a friend stops returning your texts or your child's eyes stop lighting up in your presence. It's not loud. It's not final. It's just… unfinished.

Some nights, I'd close my eyes and let the stars blur into soft, glowing tears across the sky. I'd think about the lost people, not villains, but as visitors, temporary passengers in a life I was still learning how to drive. I didn't need to drag them into my future to prove they mattered in my past.

I still loved them. That hadn't changed. But the love was quieter now. Less about hoping they'd return, and more about thanking them for showing up when they did.

Somewhere in the silence, I began to hear myself again.

And as I looked up at that swirling, imperfect sky, messy, mysterious, alive, I thought, *maybe this is what healing looks like. Not clean. Not easy. Just… true.*

The Nature of Impermanent Love

Some kinds of love do not promise forever but offer something quieter, more sacred: presence without possession. I'm learning that loving someone doesn't always mean they'll walk beside you forever. Sometimes love means watching them choose a different path and wishing them well anyway. Sometimes it means carrying the best of what you shared while releasing them from any obligation to continue sharing it.

Like stars that burn bright and drift quietly out of view, these relationships leave behind trails of warmth no longer lighting your way, but proving they were once there.

This concept is rooted in Buddhist psychology: love without clinging, care without control. Not indifference, but maturity. The understanding that love is not ownership. Letting go becomes an act of grace. And grace, I've found, is not loud. It arrives like starlight: ancient, invisible, but always reaching.

The people I've lost live on in memory not as martyrs or villains, but as flawed, complex souls who loved me the best they could, for as long as they were able. I don't need to villainize them to justify my choices, just as I don't need to minimize my truth to preserve their comfort. *We can both be right to be who we are and right to want different things.*

This is the gift of duality. The sky, after all, holds both darkness and stars.

A DIFFERENT KIND OF LOVE

But even so, I love them. Quietly. Fully. From afar.

This love no longer wears the shape of need. It does not pace or plead. It simply *is*. It's a love that asks for nothing in return and honors what was without being imprisoned by what's lost.

And in learning to love this way without attachment, without agenda, I've discovered something unexpected: I've learned how to love myself with the same generosity I once reserved only for others.

Self-compassion, like the moon's soft light, does not demand attention. It illuminates in silence. I've learned to hold space for all the versions of myself, including the one who stayed hidden for so long out of fear of exactly this kind of loss.

He was not weak. *He was surviving.* And now, he's evolving.

I realize this is the beginning of reparenting. I am giving myself the words I waited to hear, the kindness I gave away but never received, the forgiveness.

TEACHERS IN THE ABSENCE

The ghosts that stay behind aren't haunting me anymore. *They're teaching me.* About love, yes, but also about courage. About authenticity. About the strange alchemy that transforms loss into wisdom.

They remind me that some departures make space for arrivals, that some endings are actually beginnings in disguise, and that when silence fills the room once held by another's laughter, it doesn't mean you've lost everything. Sometimes, it means there's room now to hear your own voice.

The pain didn't vanish, but it changed. It became soil, and from that soil, something real has begun to grow.

And so, I carry them with me not as burdens, but as teachers, not as evidence of what I've lost, but as proof of what I've been capable of loving. They've made me who I am. Even in their absence. *Especially* in their absence.

In the end, maybe that's enough.

Maybe that's everything.

Writing this chapter of my life is itself a therapeutic act.

This chapter isn't just a goodbye, it's a declaration.

I am worthy of love. Not despite my truth, but because of it.

And for anyone reading who's felt the sting of an unspoken goodbye, let this be a reminder: Your truth is not too much, your authenticity is not a liability, and you *are not alone.*

STARRY NIGHT

Van Gogh once looked out from the window of his asylum and painted the world not as it was but as he could only see it: swirls of wind, moons that breathed, stars that trembled. His pain spilled onto the canvas as something *otherworldly*.

To many, it looked strange. Too bold. Too wild. But he wasn't painting their world. He was painting *his*.

I think of that when I think of my own thoughts. These aching truths, ghosted memories, and starlit fragments of who I am are not flaws. They are brushstrokes. They are mine.

I don't see the world like everyone else. But maybe that's the point.

Like Van Gogh, I have finally permitted myself to live inside the art of my own becoming, to love the ghosts, to treasure the pain, to hold the contradictions and call them *beautiful*.

And in that strange, imperfect vision, I have found peace.

CHAPTER 14

THE QUIET ACHE NO ONE SAW

Before I could write this chapter, I wrestled with a question I didn't know how to answer: How do you name a wound that has no visible scar? How do you write a song for sadness that hums so quietly beneath the surface that no one ever hears it? I didn't know what to call the ache that had lived inside me for years. I only knew it was there, quietly shaping every part of me.

I kept searching for a metaphor, a container, a frame that could hold the full complexity of my truth without simplifying it. I looked at nature, human things, and myself. And in the small, everyday imperfections of the world, I began to see something familiar: a chipped teacup, a scuffed floorboard, a faded letter, flawed things, honest things. And then I came across a photograph of a broken ceramic bowl held together by thin, gold veins.

It was Kintsugi.

The Japanese art of repairing broken pottery uses lacquer mixed with powdered gold, silver, or platinum. This philosophy treats breakage and repair as part of an object's history, not something to be hidden but something to be celebrated.

And just like that, I knew how to tell this story.

This is the story of cracks no one saw. Of gold that no one expected. Of how my life became a vessel fractured by performance, fear, and exhaustion, and how I've slowly begun to fill those breaks with something true.

THE LONELINESS OF BEING KNOWN WRONG

There's a special kind of loneliness that doesn't come from isolation, but from being misunderstood in full view. From being seen so often, and so wrongly, that you begin to disappear behind the image of yourself you've built to survive.

To the world, I was the bright one. The social one. The one who always showed up. The laugh that floated above the noise, the hands that held casseroles and carried burdens that weren't mine. I knew everyone's birthdays. I remembered asking about their children, surgeries, and weekend plans. I was warm. I was useful. I was everything I was supposed to be.

No one ever asked what it cost.

No one saw that the shine was a glaze covering hairline fractures and cracks I couldn't afford to let show. If they saw the truth beneath the shimmer, would they still believe I belonged?

I had become a vessel that was shaped by expectation and glazed in approval. My cracks weren't obvious, but they were deep. And I carried them like secrets, hidden beneath a practiced smile.

The Architecture of Illusion

That version of me, the one everyone adored, wasn't born. He was built.

I constructed him like an architect drafting blueprints for a house I could never live in. Every joke, every compliment, every knowing glance was a calculated beam in a structure made to withstand scrutiny. But it wasn't shelter. It was a theater.

My laughter was timed, not spontaneous. My calm was curated, not real. I wore comfort like a costume. No one noticed it didn't fit.

At some point, I stopped knowing where the mask ended, and I began. The performance became so practiced, so natural, that I forgot I was acting. But I was. I was a performing man, a performing friend, a performing happy, a performing perfect.

And like fine porcelain sealed too quickly, the mask hardened before I could scream from behind it.

I displayed my achievements like trophies in a museum, cold, glossy, untouchable. Career, family, marriage, and community were all perfect exhibits in a curated life. But I wasn't living in that life. I was ghosting through it, polishing its windows while crumbling inside.

Because even perfection when it is false becomes its own kind of pain.

THE TERROR OF DISCOVERY

The scariest part wasn't that no one saw me.

It was that I couldn't afford for them to.

Vulnerability felt like standing naked in a snowstorm. It wasn't just exposure, it was danger. A risk I had learned, too young and too often, was never worth taking.

So, I became an escape artist, a magician of misdirection. Conversations deflected. Emotions redirected authenticity, buried under hospitality and humor. Whenever someone came close to noticing the crack in my voice, I gave them something else to admire, something shiny, something easier to hold.

Because I wasn't just afraid of being rejected.

I was afraid of being truly known.

What if they looked into the bowl of my life and saw only damage? What if they saw the fracture lines and not the hands that tried so hard to hold it together? What if they discovered the man they loved was a character I'd been forced to play?

So, I kept the mask on, even in private, especially in private, until it stopped being a mask at all and became my skin.

But even skin cracks, eventually.

THE CRESCENDO OF ISOLATION

The thing about cracks is that at first, we try to hide them. We smooth them down, paint over them, pretend the surface was never broken. But over time, the effort of hiding becomes heavier than the fracture itself. That's when you realize: maybe the healing isn't in the hiding at all. Maybe it's in choosing to see the break, honor it, and fill it with gold.

That's what loneliness taught me, not the kind that comes from being alone, but the kind that grows loudest in a room full of people who think they know you. It is the ache of being misnamed, misread, misunderstood… while smiling, serving, and nodding at stories you no longer recognize.

This ache didn't scream. It hummed quietly beneath every "I'm good, how are you?" It echoed in the car ride home from parties where I was told how radiant I was. And I was radiant because performance is a kind of light. But light can burn, too.

I had become a porcelain version of myself: polished, admired, displayed. But the pressure of perfection was beginning to splinter.

The Weight of Wrong Living

Somewhere along the way, I realized I was living a life meant for someone else's body. Each day felt like trying to zip a dress two sizes too small, forcing myself to contort, smile, and fit.

I was cast in a role I never auditioned for. The script was handed to me long ago: "Be helpful, be kind, be agreeable, be enough." I memorized my lines like survival depended on them, and in some ways, it did.

But behind every achievement, polished photo, and celebration, a part of me whispered, *this isn't it.* That whisper became a fracture. And the fracture grew.

But I didn't want to shatter. I just wanted to breathe without performing. To exist without editing. To be loved without earning it in applause.

Kintsugi doesn't throw away the broken bowl. It doesn't pretend the cracks never happened. It says *this mattered. This broke. And this will be made beautiful not despite the break, but because of it.*

That is what I was beginning to want. Not erasure. Not reinvention. Repair. With gold.

A Message for the One Still Hiding

To the one still hiding

The one still stitching smiles into their face each morning like armor.

The one calculating each word in conversations, translating truth into safety, joy into palatability.

I see you.

I see the tightness in your shoulders, the breath you hold before entering rooms where everyone assumes you're fine. I see the mask that once protected you, but now cuts into your skin in places only you can feel. I know the strange ache of being loved for a version of yourself you no longer recognize.

I know what it feels like to wonder if the love you receive would remain if you stopped performing.

But hear me: you are not too much.

Your cracks do not make you less whole. They prove you have lived, endured, stretched, bent, and survived. Your breaking didn't ruin you. It revealed you.

If you ever choose to step into the light with your real self, unguarded and unedited, you will not be starting from scratch. You will be walking forward as something rarer than perfect: repaired, honest, golden.

THE GOLDEN THREAD

They say when something shatters, you can hear the break. But not every fracture is loud. Some happen silently, beneath the surface, like porcelain hairline cracks that don't scream but split you.

I didn't explode. I eroded.

Like river stones worn down by unseen currents, my edges smoothed by years of pleasing, performing, pretending. I had become glossy and palatable, easy to hold until I finally slipped through my own fingers.

That's how the mask fell not with drama, but with gravity.

And that's when I remembered Kintsugi.

Not as a metaphor. As a mirror.

Because the moment you stop trying to be whole by hiding your breaks is when you begin to heal with intention. Kintsugi doesn't erase the cracks; it makes them visible. It is golden, worth showing. It tells you *you are not broken. You are proof that mending is sacred work.*

THE TORMENT OF MISALIGNMENT

The world may never understand the quiet torment of living a life you were never meant for. They see your highlight reel and mistake it for peace. They praise the version of you they recognize, not realizing they're applauding the costume, not the soul beneath it.

What they don't see is the internal surveillance system you live under, the constant vigilance it takes to uphold a character you never meant to play. Every word is filtered, every emotion revised, and every gesture measured.

I had made a life of loving people who could only love a version of me that required my daily self-abandonment. And no, maybe it wasn't their fault. They loved the performance because I never gave them a backstage pass.

But the cost? The cost was the slow starvation of my own soul. The loss of breath. The weight of silence presses against my ribs.

I wasn't just tired. I was disappearing.

I had become a mosaic of everyone else's expectations held together by fear, not love.

The Promise on the Other Side

But here's what I discovered on the other side of the fracture: freedom is worth the loss.

Yes, the price was high. I lost relationships I thought would carry me through life. I was misunderstood by people who once adored me. I felt the sting of rejection from those whose opinions I had once bent my spine to protect.

But with that loss came something else: the ability to exhale for the first time in years. To walk through a room without adjusting my essence. To speak one sentence that didn't need editing between my heart and mouth.

To look in the mirror and *finally recognize myself again*.

That was worth more than approval. More than comfort. More than the illusion of belonging.

Because now, I belonged to me.

Even If You Lose Everything

Even if you lose everything that once made you feel valuable, the roles, the praise, the certainty, there is something you will gain that no one can take from you:

The stillness of truth.

The breath that doesn't tremble.

The gold running through every visible crack.

And yes, some people may never understand. Some may only know how to love the edited version of you, the well-lit photograph, the carefully arranged narrative. Let them go. Let them carry their idea of you, while you carry your truth.

You were never made to be flawless. You were made to be real.

THE TRUTH ABOUT BROKENNESS

Let me say it clearly now:
You were never broken.

You were buried.
You were layered in obligations.
You were covered in the dust of other people's desires.
But you? You were always whole underneath.

The version of you feeling "too much" was *just right*. The one who hid because she didn't fit was exactly what the world needed. You don't need to restart your life from scratch; you just need to honor the parts that already survived.

Let the cracks stay. Fill them with gold. Let them glisten. Let them catch the light.

Because *that* is where your power lives.

THE TIME TO RISE

And so, whenever you're ready, not when it's convenient or safe or guaranteed, when *you're* ready: rise.

Rise gently, not like fire but like breath.

Like warm lacquer seeping into the fractures of a life, solidifying, gleaming, saying: *I'm still here.*

Let your rising be quiet or loud, slow or sudden, but let it be yours. No performance. No apology.

Your freedom is not in becoming someone new; it's in returning to the person you've always been beneath the debris.

That self is waiting.

That self is worthy.

That self has never stopped believing in you.

To Anyone Reading This

If you've ever felt invisible while being celebrated, if you've worn smiles like armor and applause like chains…

If you've performed joy while grieving your own disappearance…

Please know: *your truth is not too much.*

Your cracks are not your flaw. They are your proof of becoming.

And you are still becoming.

Always.

CHAPTER 15

LOVING THE GHOSTS THAT STAY BEHIND

THE LOVE THAT OUTLIVED THE LIVING

There are some wounds that time does not heal; it teaches you how to carry them. You learn their weight the way you learn a limp: unconsciously, awkwardly, always aware of the ache beneath your skin. They do not scab over. They do not scar neatly. Instead, they live within you, reshaping the hollows of your chest and the quiet hours of your day.

Some people lose their children to death. I lost mine to silence.

Not the stillness of a coffin, no, this kind is crueler. This kind walks and breathes and celebrates birthdays. It posts photos online. It thrives in rooms you are no longer allowed to enter.

No one brings casseroles when your children vanish from your life while still being alive. There's no funeral for estrangement. No obituary for a mother whose name is erased quietly, as if it never belonged on their lips to begin with.

What I didn't understand then was how grief without closure becomes a kind of psychological purgatory suspended between hope and acceptance, unable to complete the natural mourning process that death provides. The mind craves finality, seeks patterns, demands meaning. Ambiguous loss offers none of these mercies.

My boys were my world. Not metaphorically. Not poetically. Literally. Every breath I took was structured around their needs, dreams, and joys. I was not just their father, I was their gravity, and they were mine. The center around which every version of myself had learned to orbit.

In their laughter, I found my lullabies. In their footsteps, my prayers.

When they were small, love was simple, instinctive, wild, and undeserved in the best way. They didn't need me to be anything other than present. They didn't ask about my identity or notice the masks I wore. They just needed someone to kiss their scraped knees and listen when their world felt too big.

This is how enmeshment begins not with malice, but with devotion. When a parent's identity becomes so intertwined with their children's existence that boundaries dissolve, love can become a cage for both parties. I see now what I couldn't see then: that in making them my entire world, I may have made their world feel too small.

But children grow. With growth comes a new kind of vision, sharpened by culture, opinions, and what they're told love should look like. Psychologists call it individuation the necessary developmental task of becoming separate beings. What feels like rejection to a parent is often a child's desperate attempt to discover who they are beyond our expectations, our dreams, our overwhelming love.

And suddenly, the person who once read them bedtime stories in silly voices becomes too much. Too different. Too complicated. A fracture in the image of who they believed you were.

And so, they vanish. Not loudly. Not with screaming or broken plates. But with a slow withdrawal. Missed calls. Neutral texts. Short answers. Distance disguised as maturity.

You realize you are a ghost haunting the edges of their new lives.

The Quiet Ritual of Letting Go

The hardest part of this grief is that they are still here. Somewhere. Laughing. Living. Unwilling to look back.

But I did not let go. Not at first. Hope, that stubborn, holy thing, burrowed into my bones like marrow. It kept whispering: maybe not today, but soon. Maybe not this silence, but something softer might follow.

Hope, I learned, can be both medicine and poison. Attachment theory teaches us that secure bonds create resilience, but anxious attachment the kind born of fear and scarcity creates a clinging that strangles what it seeks to preserve. I was living in what therapists call "complicated grief," mourning someone who wasn't dead, loving someone who felt unreachable.

So, I reached out. Again, and again. I became fluent in the language of gentle persistence. Birthday cards without heavy words. Text messages that said, "Thinking of you," but never "Why won't you answer?" Gifts left quietly at doorsteps, timed with holidays and milestones reminders that I still remembered every date, every detail.

Sometimes, there was a flicker of response. A short thank-you. A practical request, a favor, a reference, a signature. Parent things. Things that used to be so automatic, so everyday, but now felt like miracles. Like cracks of light beneath a locked door.

These intermittent reinforcements are what keep us hooked random rewards that psychologists know create the strongest behavioral patterns. Like gamblers at slot machines, I was addicted to the possibility of connection, each small response feeding the hunger for more while leaving me fundamentally unsatisfied.

In those moments, I let myself imagine: Maybe this is how we begin again. Maybe we can find our way back in tiny gestures, like building a bridge one stone at a time.

I went to events when invited, or when I thought I could blend into the background without drawing discomfort. Graduations. Weddings. Moments where I was not the center but still allowed to witness. And I clung to every polite smile like it was evidence proof that the door was not entirely closed.

But hope, when stretched too thin across too much silence, becomes something else. Not strength. Not endurance. But mourning. A slow kind of grief that masquerades as faith.

There's a psychological term for this: "disenfranchised grief" mourning that society doesn't recognize or validate. Unlike death, estrangement carries shame. People assume you must have done something wrong, that love should be enough, that good parents don't lose their children this way. The isolation compounds the loss.

There's a particular weight in loving people who no longer reach back. A fatigue that settles into your spirit when you realize you are writing letters to a version of the past. The people you remember aren't the ones standing in the present. And maybe, just maybe, you aren't the person they remember either.

This was my first glimpse of wisdom: We don't love people; we love our experience of them. We love the stories we tell ourselves about who they are, the memories we've curated, the versions of them that live in our minds. When those people change or when we're forced to see them clearly we must grieve not just the relationship, but our own illusions.

The energy I was spending on hope was no longer sustainable. My children had become ideas I was clinging to rather than individuals with their own agency and choices. I was loving phantoms people I once knew, people I raised, now reshaped by distance and decision and a story I was no longer invited to narrate.

The reaching began to slow. Not out of bitterness, but out of truth. Even love needs oxygen. And this love was holding its breath.

Radical acceptance isn't a feeling, it's practice. It's the daily choice to stop fighting reality, even when reality feels unbearable.

Buddhist philosophy teaches that suffering comes not from pain itself, but from our resistance to pain. I was learning to feel the ache without trying to fix it, to love without demanding love in return.

So, I sat in the silence. Let it ring in my ears. Not as punishment, but as clarity. Because sometimes, choosing peace means releasing the hand you've been holding in your imagination. Sometimes, it means admitting that the echo is not a reply. It's just an echo.

I began to write less. I stopped marking holidays with reminders of my presence. I still thought of them daily, but I let those thoughts float instead of gripping them. I did not chase.

And still I loved them. Still, I love them. But love that clings begins to rot. So, I laid mine down softly. Not in surrender. But in sacred release.

This is what mature love looks like: loving someone enough to let them be who they choose to be, even when that choice doesn't include you. It's love without ownership, connection without attachment, care without control. It took losing them to learn how to truly love them.

THE SHAPE OF WHAT REMAINS

This grief is not linear. It loops and curves and folds back on itself. It doesn't ask for permission or give warning. It just arrives, uninvited, and sits beside me like it owns the place. And in many ways, it does.

Trauma rewires the brain, creates neural pathways that trigger without warning. A song, a scent, a stranger's laugh can flood the nervous system with memories, as if the past is happening now. Healing isn't about erasing these pathways it's about learning to witness them with compassion rather than being overwhelmed by them.

Some days, I barely think of what I've lost. I make it through morning coffee, emails, headlines, and dishes in the sink without the ache announcing itself. But then something small a song, a smell, a memory triggered by nothing I can trace will land like a stone in my chest, and I'll remember all over again.

I grieve them in grocery aisles when I pass by their favorite foods. I grieve them in back-to-school commercials and in the voice of a child calling "Dad!" that isn't meant for me. I grieve them in laughter that sounds like theirs and in the quiet that follows when I realize it isn't.

I used to dream about reconciliation the moment the phone rang and I heard their voices again. I imagined the tears, the apologies, the reunion years compressed into one fragile embrace. But that dream has softened with time, its edges dulled by reality. I've stopped hoping for a moment; instead, I hope for peace for them, for me, for something that doesn't ask us to go back, only forward.

Recovery rarely looks like restoration. More often, it looks like integration taking the broken pieces and creating something new. Post-traumatic growth is real: many who survive profound loss discover strengths they never knew they had, develop deeper empathy, find meaning they couldn't access before the shattering.

This isn't the kind of healing you notice all at once. It's not a grand crescendo or triumphant declaration. It's quiet, steady, and often invisible. It looks like breath returning to the body. It looks like setting the table for one without feeling the need to apologize. It looks like planting something new in a garden that once only held memories.

I learned that identity is not fixed, it's fluid, renewable, capable of reconstruction. For years, "dad" had been my primary self-definition. Losing that role forced me to excavate other parts of myself: the writer who had been silenced, the dreamer who had been deferred, the man who existed independent of his relationships to others.

And maybe that's what healing really is not the erasure of pain, but the integration of it. A way of carrying the absence without letting it define the whole. A way of loving someone without losing yourself to the ache of it.

So now I wake up and do the things that bring me back to myself. I write. I walk. I talk to the sky. I love the people who show up, and I hold space for the ones who don't. And I remind myself, when the grief returns, and it always does, that I survived the kind of silence that could have swallowed me whole.

Self-compassion becomes the antidote to shame. Where I once asked, "What did I do wrong?" I learned to ask "What did I learn?" Where I once saw failure, I began to see a fierce father's love that, while imperfect, was real and powerful and worthy of honor.

I am left tracing their shape in photos that once held warmth but now feel like cold glass. I keep them framed anyway. Because love doesn't disappear when it becomes invisible.

The paradox of letting go is that it often brings us closer to what we've lost than clinging ever could. When I stopped demanding their presence, I could finally feel their influence. They live in my resilience, my capacity for joy, my ability to love others without suffocating them. They live in every lesson I learned from loving them, even the painful ones.

FOR THE ONES LEFT HOLDING THE SILENCE

You who sit in empty rooms, setting plates for voices that do not come you, are not forgotten.

You who whisper love into voids, who mourn what lives but will not speak, you are not alone.

There is strength in staying soft. There is grace in grieving without an audience. There is beauty in bearing witness to what once was and still choosing to live anyway.

And there is wisdom in knowing this: You can love someone completely and still not be what they need. You can do your best and still have it not be enough. You can be a good parent and still lose your children to forces beyond your control. Your worth is not measured by their presence. Your love is not diminished by their absence.

This is the hardest truth and the most liberating one: We are not responsible for other people's choices, only for our response to them. In that response lies our power, our dignity, and our capacity for transformation.

135

CHAPTER 16

THE GARDEN I DIDN'T KNOW I WAS PLANTING

THE MYTH OF THE CLEAN SLATE

There was a time when I believed healing meant departure. To move forward, I had to erase everything behind me. I imagined myself stepping into some sterile, untouched future, one scrubbed clean of mistakes, losses, grief, and regret. Like wiping a whiteboard of everything that had ever been written, hoping the absence would somehow feel like freedom.

I mistook healing for performance.

I treated transformation like a checklist: therapy sessions, affirmations, and scheduled breakthroughs. If I could just complete enough emotional to-do lists, I would be reborn, stronger, shinier, and new.

But healing, I've come to understand, isn't an escape route. It's not a sprint toward a cleaner version of myself. It's the slow turning of soil, the remembering of roots. It's not the abandonment of the past, but the careful folding of it into the future. My life wasn't meant to be scrubbed clean; it was meant to be replanted.

I didn't learn this in a triumphant moment. There was no cinematic breakthrough, no grand epiphany. The truth met me gently, like morning mist settling over a quiet field. I was alone in my home, the room silent except for the sound of my breathing, when I felt it, that curious paradox Carl Rogers once described: *"When I accept myself just as I am, then I can change."*

It stopped me.

There was no fanfare, no burst of light. Just stillness. And in that stillness, something began to shift.

THE QUIET ACHE NO ONE SAW

For years, I had performed happiness like a play I couldn't exit. I knew my lines. I knew when to smile, how to glow on cue. I hosted dinners like they were opening nights. I stood beside others like a supporting character in their stories. People praised the version of me I presented, the dependable one, the lighthearted one, the man who could hold any room with ease.

There's a special kind of loneliness that doesn't come from being alone. It comes from being surrounded by laughter, by love, by people who think they know you and you still feel invisible. It's the ache of being misunderstood while performing a version of yourself that everyone applauds.

To the outside world, I was magnetic. The easy laugh. The warm hug. The one who remembered birthdays and brought wine to dinner. I filled rooms with conversation, cheered loudest at my boys' games, and smiled like joy was stitched into my skin. I looked exactly how people expected me to look: happy, fulfilled, grounded.

But that version of me was a curated illusion. Every smile I wore was a patch over panic. Every laugh, a distraction from the quiet unraveling underneath.

When the curtain closed, and the guests had gone, I would sit on the edge of my bed, wondering who that man really was. The one I performed, or the one staring blankly at the wall, too numb to move.

The exhaustion wasn't sudden. It was slow erosion. Like wind carving stone, day by day, moment by moment. I had chipped away at myself for years, smiling through sorrow, nodding through emptiness, until I barely recognized the silhouette I'd become.

I stacked achievements like armor, proof that I was okay. That I was thriving. But none of it was about fulfillment. It was about survival. About keeping the truth buried beneath layers of performance. Because the truth was fragile. And I was terrified that if anyone saw it, they'd walk away.

THE FIRST CRACK IN THE MASK

I remember the moment the mask slipped for the first time just for a second. It was a cool evening. I had just come home from a work trip. My youngest was sitting at the kitchen table, doing homework. He looked up and asked, "Why are you sad?"

I froze.

I hadn't said a word. I hadn't sighed or frowned. But something in me had leaked through the cracks. I laughed it off, kissed his forehead, and said, "I'm just tired, son." But inside, I was shaken. He saw me. Not the version I curated, he saw *me*.

That evening, I went for a run to clear my head and emotions, and when I returned, I cried in the shower. Not because I was sad but because I realized how deeply I'd buried myself. Even my children only knew the mask.

Months later, I stood in front of that same mirror, preparing for another business trip. I had the proper outfit, everything was packed. The practiced smile was on my face. But something inside me snapped.

I stared at my reflection and whispered, "I don't know who you are."

It wasn't dramatic. No screaming. No shattered glass. Just a quiet reckoning. A moment where the performance felt unbearable. I sat on the edge of the tub and asked myself the question I'd been avoiding for years:

"What would happen if I stopped pretending?"

The answer terrified me. But it also lit a spark.

THE RECKONING BENEATH THE SURFACE

And so, with dirt still beneath my nails from that first brave turn of the soil, I began to live differently, not louder, not bolder, but truer.

I had imagined healing would arrive with fireworks, applause, and some grand scene of liberation. Instead, it came quietly, like watching seeds under the surface, nothing visible at first, but everything changing in the dark. The performance I had sustained for years didn't collapse with a crash. It dissolved, slowly, in silence. And in that silence, I began to hear myself for the first time.

In a hotel room that evening, alone with my thoughts, I wrote myself a letter in my journal:

Dear Me,

I know you're tired. I know you think you must keep smiling, keep achieving, keep showing up as someone you're not. I know you believe that if you stop, everything will fall apart.

But listen to me: your truth is not a threat. It's a lifeline.

You don't have to earn love by being perfect. You don't have to hide your pain to protect others. You are allowed to be seen. Fully. Fiercely. Flawed.

One day, you'll look in the mirror and see someone you recognize. Someone you love. Someone free.

Hold on. The ache won't last forever.

LOVE, THE YOU WHO FINALLY CHOSE HIMSELF.

But I wasn't alone in this ache. It's everywhere. It's in the mother who smiles through postpartum depression because she's afraid to be labeled unstable. It's in the executive who climbs the ladder but feels emptier with every promotion. It's in the teenager who laughs with friends but cries alone at night, wondering if anyone truly sees them. It's in the man who's been taught that emotions are weakness, so he swallows his grief until it hardens into silence.

We are a society of performers. But behind every mask is a story, a truth, a soul aching to be known.

ROOM FOR THE ROOTS TO BREATHE

I had to admit that to myself: "The person who could illuminate every room had forgotten how to find light alone."

The loneliness of being unseen, *truly unseen*, didn't howl. It hummed beneath everything like a low, relentless drone. Fog across a familiar field. Soft. Invasive. I hadn't recognized how lost I was because I was always in motion. Productivity had been my hiding place. Performance, my armor.

But now, sitting still in a quiet room, I faced a deeper truth: I had spent so long running toward "better" that I never once looked back with tenderness. I treated my past like a stain to scrub out. But what if it wasn't a stain at all? What if it was the compost?

It was in that stillness, uncluttered by obligation and unmasked from expectation, that something remarkable happened. I began to see fragments of myself not as failures but as clues. There was no singular "me" I needed to become, just someone I needed to *remember*.

That's when I stumbled into something radical: self-compassion.

Dr. Kristin Neff called it "giving ourselves the same kindness and care we'd offer a good friend." But what do you do when you've never offered yourself a kind word? When your inner voice is made of sharp corners and cold silence?

For years, I had been brutal with myself. You don't even recognize the brutal as cruelty because it's been your native tongue. Every mistake became a moral failing. Every slow day was a weakness. I held myself to impossible standards, and when I failed to meet them, I turned that failure into identity.

But self-compassion is a different kind of seed. And it doesn't bloom loudly. It unfurls shyly. Hesitantly. It's the sprout you nearly step on because you weren't expecting anything to grow.

"Healing didn't demand perfection," I wrote one day in my journal, "it asked for presence."

So, I started writing. Not essays. Not anything polished. Just honesty, raw and unedited. I wrote letters I never sent. I filled pages with grief that had waited years to be named. I wrote without the need to make sense, just to make space.

And in those pages, I started to hear something… *my voice.*

Not the one crafted for comfort or cloaked in charm. The *real* one. It was shaky at first, unsure if it was allowed to speak without consequence. But it spoke anyway.

Eventually, I shared some of that truth with someone close. I was terrified. Vulnerability always felt like exposure, and exposure had always meant risk. But they stayed. They didn't turn away, correct, or console. They *listened.*

And when I cried, it wasn't because I was broken. It was because I was finally *known.*

That moment, that tender staying, was the first crack in the old performance. And for once, I didn't rush to repair it.

Instead, I let the light in.

THE SACRED GROUND OF IDENTITY

Somewhere between the silence I stopped apologizing for and the journal pages I filled without judgment, I noticed something shift. Not a breakthrough. Not a "healed" stamp pressed on my chest. Just... space. A loosening. Like the roots of something long-constrained finally found room to stretch into softer ground.

For the first time in years, I wasn't rushing toward improvement or clawing toward anyone else's expectations. I was letting the ground be what it was and letting myself be.

Healing didn't feel noble. It felt like confusion some days and emptiness on others. But it was mine, and that made it sacred. My grief no longer needed to be edited to be palatable. It could sit beside my joy without apology, like old friends who didn't speak often but always made room at the table.

"I was never broken. I was just unheard, unseen, misunderstood."

But identity, I've learned, is not a mask we wear, it's our face beneath it. It's not a role we play; it's the quiet truth we return to when no one's watching. Erik Erikson described identity as a lifelong process, shaped through crisis and resolution. That resonated deeply. Because it wasn't until I allowed the crisis to unfold, until I stopped resisting the unraveling, that I began to understand who I really was.

I am not the sum of my accomplishments, nor the shadow of my mistakes. I am not defined by who I was when I was hurting, nor by who others needed me to be. My identity is fluid, evolving, and deeply rooted in the choices I make now: to be honest, to be present, to be kind to myself.

Reclaiming my identity wasn't about finding something lost. It was about choosing consciously and gently who I wanted to be moving forward. It was about honoring the parts of me that had survived, even when they were never seen.

LOVE THAT HOLDS, NOT FIXES

In this slower season, I discovered a different kind of love a love that didn't ask me to shrink or pretend. He saw me fully past the debris of my old identity, through the scars and silences I used to hide behind. He stayed. Not because I had to win him over or perform for his affection. He stayed because he wanted to know the version of me that I was still discovering.

His love was steady unshaken by my silence, unthreatened by my shadows.

He never rushed my process. He didn't yank me toward optimism when I sank into old griefs. He sat with me there, offering warmth, not advice. And when I laughed, truly laughed, it wasn't relief from pain. It was gratitude for being fully seen.

According to attachment theory, this kind of bond creates a secure base, a foundation from which we can explore the world and ourselves. I didn't have to choose between being held and being free. I could have both.

This reflects what Self-Determination Theory calls the essential ingredients of psychological well-being: autonomy, competence, and relatedness. In this relationship, I felt free to be myself, capable in my own skin, and deeply connected. Identity wasn't a threat—it was a gift.

We didn't merge into one indistinguishable soul; we stood side by side, distinct yet deeply connected. We became one in purpose, in devotion, in trust but never at the cost of our individuality. Our differences didn't divide us; they deepened us. And in that space, I discovered that the most powerful love is the one that sees you, holds you, and still lets you be you.

I stopped measuring love by how much of myself I had to erase to keep it. Instead, I began to understand that true intimacy isn't losing yourself in another but being loved more deeply *because* you remain yourself. It was unity without uniformity, a bond that honored difference and allowed expansion.

Friendships Reclaimed, Not Rekindled

Something else happened, slowly and quietly: old friendships reappeared. Not out of obligation or nostalgia, but because the energy had shifted. People who once knew me in fragments returned, not to rehash old versions of me, but to meet the one I had become.

We renewed the relationships we once enjoyed, but now the relationship was grounded in authenticity. There was no need to perform, no fear of being misunderstood. These friendships became mirrors, not of who I used to be, but of how far I'd come. And in allowing them to genuinely know the real me, I discovered new layers of growth. Their acceptance gave me the courage to stand more firmly in my truth, and their reflections helped me see the strength I hadn't realized I'd gained.

We didn't need to pretend. We could laugh at what used to be without forcing ourselves to fit those outdated roles again. It wasn't about reclaiming who I was. It was about honoring how far I'd come. These friendships mirrored my growth… soft, weathered, and stronger for the time apart.

THE DIVINE IN THE BECOMING

And God, how different that relationship became. Not the distant judge I once feared, but the gentle whisper in my spirit reminding me: *"You are mine. You are enough. You are loved."*

For most of my life, I saw God through a lens of fear. Not awe. Not reverence. Fear. He was a distant figure, majestic, yes, but unreachable. I imagined Him watching from above, clipboard in hand, measuring my worth against impossible standards. Every misstep felt like a mark against me. Every failure, a confirmation that I wasn't enough.

So, I performed. I perfected. I pretended.

There was one place, one person, who offered a different lens. As a child, I spent summers in Tennessee with my grandmother.

She had grounded faith, the kind that didn't shout but whispered truth. Balanced. Gentle. Unshaken. We'd sit on the swing on her porch at night, the stars overhead, the crickets singing their lullaby. And we'd talk about God. Not the God of judgment, but the God of unconditional love. She would always remind me: "He loves you just as you are. Unconditionally. And He'll guide you into becoming the person you were created to be."

I used to pray out of obligation, out of fear. I thought I had to earn grace, perform worthiness, prove devotion. But grace doesn't work that way. It's not a transaction, it's a gift. And love from God isn't conditional, it's eternal.

It wasn't until later during my "becoming" that something shifted. Not in the heavens, but in me. It wasn't dramatic. No lightning bolt. No booming voice. Just quiet, in the stillness, when the noise of shame finally settled, I heard something I'd never heard before. Not thunder… Not judgment… Just a whisper.

A whisper that spoke to the core of my being and said: **"You are mine. You are enough. You are loved."** I didn't read it in a book. I didn't hear it in a sermon. It was a soul-deep knowing. A truth that didn't demand proof, only surrender.

And in that surrender, I discovered something sacred: I am created in the image of God.

"So, God created mankind in his own image, in the image of God he created them; male and female he created them." —Genesis 1:27

Not despite who I am. Not as a mistake to be corrected. But as a reflection of divine creativity, divine intention, divine love.

Now I pray in the quiet moments when the sun spills across the floor, when a song moves me to tears, when I feel the pulse of life in my chest. Divinity is no longer confined to doctrine created by theologians or church leaders; it lives in breath, in beauty, in being. It meets me in silence, in laughter, in longing. It reminds me that I am never alone.

Love as an Offering

In this phase, love no longer functions as a transaction or performance. It became an offering. I no longer needed someone to fill the gaps inside me; I had already done the work of tending those spaces with care and patience.

Love became an invitation not a plea for belonging, but a gentle welcome into a life built on purpose. I wasn't trying to be chosen anymore. I was choosing, too.

I loved again, not to fill a void, not to silence loneliness, but to share the space I'd finally made for myself. Love became an offering, not a transaction. It was no longer about proving my worth or earning affection. It was about inviting someone into the life I had built with intention and care.

The Cost and the Gift

This journey taught me that authenticity will cost you comfort, but it will give you clarity. I learned that truth doesn't always come with applause. Sometimes it comes with silence, rejection, or the slow unraveling of relationships. But clarity is a gift.

When the fog of pretending lifts, you see who truly stands with you and who only stood with your mask.

Yes, much was lost. The deepest wound was losing my boys. That ache is timeless, tender, and unyielding. I still hear the sound of their laughter echoing down the hallway, the way their small hands fit perfectly into mine. I remember bedtime stories and whispered prayers. I dream about the many hours spent on the baseball and soccer field or the trips we enjoyed that constantly brought new experiences and laughter. Now, silence fills those spaces.

Yet I've learned that a father's love isn't defined by proximity or presence. It's a thread that runs through every breath a silent prayer wrapped in hope. If the time apart becomes forever, my heart will still hold space for them always. I still dream of a day when they'll ask, "Why?" and I'll answer with truth, love, and open arms.

But what bloomed in place of what was lost was richer than anything I could have imagined. New companions stepped into my life not to replace the old, but to remind me that love is fluid, connection is resilient, and belonging is never singular.

The Garden That Had Always Been There

Looking back, I see it now: I had been planting a garden all along. Every act of courage, small truth told, and tear shed in solitude was a seed. And this quiet, sturdy life is my harvest.

The garden you didn't know you were planting has been growing all along, fed by every moment of courage, every act of self-compassion. It is beautiful, not despite the struggle, but because of it.

There are still shadows. There are still unanswered questions. But I no longer mistake that for failure. I no longer believe peace only belongs to those who have it all figured out.

Peace, I've learned, belongs to those who allow themselves to bloom—slowly, imperfectly, but fully.

THE INVITATION TO BEGIN

And now, standing here, not fully bloomed but certainly rooted, I want to extend that same invitation:

You don't need a dramatic collapse to begin. You only need a quiet moment of honesty, a willingness to listen to the voice you've drowned out with busyness and obligation.

Let go of the idea that healing is a performance. It isn't. It's presence. Let go of the idea that vulnerability is weakness. It's the soil where everything real begins.

You don't have to rush your way to wholeness. There's no prize for finishing fast. This is not a race. It's a slow bloom.

Start where you are. Let go of the need to perform. Let go of the belief that healing must look like strength. Instead, choose softness. Choose truth. Choose to honor the parts of you that have survived, even when they were never seen.

Begin to memorialize the beauty in your own story—not to live in it, but to learn from it. Let your past become fertile ground for something new. Let your identity be something you shape with intention, not something you inherit from expectation.

Because when you choose to meet yourself with compassion, when you stop chasing perfection and start embracing presence, something shifts. You begin to feel lighter. You begin to feel real. You begin to feel free.

The cost of authenticity is high, but the cost of denial is higher. Living a lie drains the soul. It erodes joy, distorts relationships, and leaves you chasing shadows.

Truth, on the other hand, is terrifying. It threatens comfort. It risks rejection. It demands courage. But truth is also the only thing that heals. It may hurt in the moment, but it liberates in the long run. It clears the fog. It invites real love, real joy, real connection.

And the benefit? It's not just healing, it's wholeness. It's waking up and knowing you are enough, not just someday, not when you've earned it, but now. It's the quiet joy of being fully alive in your own skin.

So, plant your garden. Tend to it gently. Let it grow in its own time. And when the first bloom appears, fragile, radiant, unmistakably yours, you'll know this is what it means to come home to yourself.

And so, I keep tending. I keep showing up, not for the illusion of perfection, but for the reality of becoming. I am the gardener now. And this life, this self, this truth was worth waiting for.

You were never broken. You were only buried. And now, it's time to rise. Whenever you're ready.

CHAPTER 17

WE ARE CREATED IN HIS IMAGE

*"Your identity is not earned. It is divine,
enduring, and unconditional."*

Throughout this book, I have walked you through the most profound reconciliation of my life, a careful, often painful process of coming to terms with truths I had spent decades avoiding. I have reconciled with myself, learning to accept the person I am rather than the person I thought I should be. I have reconciled with the complex realities of relationship, accepting both the devastating losses that came with choosing authenticity and the unexpected gains that emerged from living truthfully.

But there remained one final reconciliation, perhaps the most important of all: coming to terms with God.

Faith has always been woven into the fabric of who I am. Even in my deepest struggles with identity and belonging, even when religious institutions felt unsafe and spiritual communities became sources of pain rather than comfort, I could never fully walk away from the sense that there was something sacred at the center of existence, something that called to me, challenged me, and ultimately held me.

Yet for most of my life, my understanding of God had been filtered through the same lens of performance and fear that distorted everything else. The divine became another audience to impress, another source of conditional love to earn, another relationship where my authentic self felt unwelcome and unsafe.

THE GOD OF FEAR

I used to believe God had a file on me. A thick, overstuffed manila folder containing every flaw I'd tried to hide, every mistake I'd tried to forget, every shameful thought I'd tried to pray away. In my mind, heaven wasn't a sanctuary but a surveillance room, and God existed as a distant figure perched high above the chaos of human existence, watching with the cold precision of a judge measuring my worth against impossible standards.

This God kept meticulous records of my failures, maintained detailed files of my shortcomings, and waited with barely contained disappointment for me to inevitably fall short of His expectations. He demanded perfection but offered only conditional love. He required transparency but punished authenticity. He called for honesty while rewarding those who hid their struggles behind smiles and scripture verses.

What I didn't understand then was how profoundly my early attachment experiences had shaped this image of the divine. Psychologist John Bowlby's attachment theory reveals how our earliest relationships with caregivers form templates for all future relationships, including our relationship with God.

When we experience conditional love in childhood, when acceptance depends on good behavior and rejection follows disappointment, we unconsciously project these patterns onto our understanding of the divine.

I wore masks not just for the world around me, but for Him, perhaps especially for Him, because the stakes felt highest in that relationship. I had been taught, both implicitly and directly, that God's love was something you earned through obedience and lost through error. He gave affection only when I performed well, and when I didn't, He disappeared. Silence became His judgment. Distance became His punishment.

I built my faith on performance. My prayers were edited, my confessions calculated, my tears rehearsed. Even in prayer, I came to God only with what I thought He could love. And then I wondered why I always felt far away.

Theologian Henri Nouwen writes extensively about how we tend to create God in the image of our human experiences rather than recognizing ourselves as created in God's image. My fearful God was a projection of every conditional relationship I had ever known, every transaction-based love that required me to earn my place.

> *"The greatest trap in our life is not success, popularity, or power, but self-rejection."* —Henri Nouwen

THE SACRED MIRROR

There was a time I only looked into mirrors to fix something, my hair, my expression, my posture, my performance. I would stand before my reflection not to see myself but to edit myself, to filter what the world was allowed to see.

Even in prayer, I mirrored that habit: "God, here's the best of me. Please don't look too close at the rest."

I thought holiness meant invisibility. To become divine, I had to erase what made me human—the struggle, the contradictions, the wounds I kept hidden. But the closer I came to healing, the more I began to understand that holiness was never about perfection but about wholeness. And wholeness welcomes every part.

What no one told me was that shame has a voice, and if you grow up hearing it long enough, you confuse it for God's.

Shame says, "You're too much." Shame says, "You're not enough." Shame says, "Be smaller." Shame says, "You're a burden."

And God? Well, I had Him sounding just like shame. My fear wasn't just about punishment; it was about rejection. I believed that if I let myself be fully seen, even by God, I'd be left, forgotten, judged.

This performance-based spirituality aligns with what psychologists call "conditional positive regard" the message that we are only valuable when we meet certain standards. Carl Rogers identified this as one of the most damaging patterns in human development, creating what he termed "conditions of worth" that prevent us from experiencing authentic self-acceptance.

THE WHISPER THAT CHANGED EVERYTHING

During my journey of becoming, that long, difficult process of shedding false selves and discovering who I really was beneath all the performance something fundamental shifted. Not in the heavens, as if God Himself had suddenly changed His mind about me, but in my capacity to perceive what had perhaps always been true.

For most of my life, I thought spiritual transformation would feel like thunder. I waited for the heavens to crack open, imagined fire and trembling and revelation in bold print. But it came so quietly when it happened that I nearly missed it.

It came in stillness. Not when I was praying with fervor or fasting or striving. It came when I had nothing left to prove, nothing to hide, nothing rehearsed. I wasn't performing anymore. I was exhausted. Finally, still.

And in that stillness, something moved. Not outside me, within. I don't remember the day exactly, but I remember the moment. The air didn't change. The sky didn't break open. But something did.

I was sitting alone, just breathing, when the voice came, not in volume, but in weight:

You are mine. You are enough. You are loved.

Each word landed like a stone dropped in water. Simple. Undeniable. Irrevocable. Not thunder rolling across the sky or the booming voice of judgment I had always expected. Instead, it was a whisper, gentle as breath, speaking directly to the core of my being with words that seemed to come from both everywhere and nowhere at once.

This wasn't a revelation born of doctrine or dogma. It wasn't something I could trace back to a particular sermon or scripture study. It was deeper than intellectual understanding, more fundamental than theological concept. It was a soul-deep knowing, a truth that didn't demand proof or explanation, only surrender to its reality.

What I experienced aligns with what neuroscientist Antonio Damasio calls "somatic markers" the bodily felt senses of truth that operate below the level of conscious thought. This experiential knowledge reflects what the Desert Fathers called "gnosis" not intellectual information about God, but direct, transformative encounter with divine reality.

Knowing came with its own evidence not the kind you could present in an argument, but the kind that transforms you from the inside out. It was like finally hearing music after a lifetime of reading about melodies, like seeing color for the first time after years of black and white photographs.

And in that surrender, in the letting go of my need to earn what was already freely given, I discovered something sacred that had been true all along but hidden beneath layers of fear and misunderstanding: I am created in the image of God.

THE FOUNDATION OF WORTH

*"So God created mankind in his own image, in
the image of God he created them; male and
female he created them." —Genesis 1:27*

These ancient words, which I had read countless times before, suddenly carried new weight, revealed depths I had never seen. The Hebrew phrase "imago Dei" has been central to theological anthropology for centuries, yet its implications are often obscured by our tendency to reduce it to behavioral characteristics or moral qualities.

One quiet morning, sunlight slid across the hardwood floor, catching my reflection in the glass. I looked up slowly, reluctantly, and there he was this man I'd spent a lifetime avoiding. Tired eyes, slight slouch. A smile formed, not because everything was okay, but because he was still standing.

"I am not broken," I whispered. "I am beautifully and wonderfully made."

I didn't say it to convince myself. I said it because I finally believed it, not in my mind, but in my spirit.

Contemporary theologian Jürgen Moltmann argues that being created in God's image is not about what we do but about who we are, our fundamental identity as beloved creatures who reflect divine nature not through perfection but through our very existence. I began to understand that my worth wasn't contingent on my behavior, my acceptance wasn't dependent on my perfection, my belonging wasn't earned through good works.

I was created in God's image, not in spite of who I am, not as a mistake to be corrected or a problem to be solved, but as a deliberate reflection of divine creativity, divine intention, divine love. Every aspect of my being, including the parts I had learned to hide and hate, carried within it some reflection of divine nature.

Even the parts I was taught to hide:

- The part that overthinks everything
- The part that forgets to return phone calls
- The part that still doubts sometimes
- The part that needs reminders
- The part that gets overwhelmed in big crowds
- The part that cries when someone else cries
- The part that still waits to be chosen

All of it. Image-bearer. All of it. Holy.

"The wound is the place where the Light enters you." —Rumi

LAYING DOWN THE LIES

To accept this truth required laying down every lie I had ever believed about myself, every message I had internalized about my fundamental unworthiness, every story that painted me as inherently flawed or intrinsically broken.

Cognitive behavioral therapy identifies these internalized messages as "core beliefs" the fundamental assumptions about ourselves that shape how we interpret every experience. These beliefs often form in childhood and operate unconsciously, filtering reality through the lens of our earliest relational experiences.

I had to stop striving and start receiving, had to cease the relentless effort to earn love and begin the vulnerable work of accepting it as a gift. I had to stop hiding behind carefully constructed personas and start shining as the person I was actually created to be.

Carl Jung reminds us that "The privilege of a lifetime is to become who you truly are." In discovering my identity as one created in God's image, I began to understand that becoming who I truly was wasn't rebellion against the divine it was alignment with divine intention. Authenticity wasn't sin; it was sacred duty.

There's a kind of miracle that doesn't come with lightning or signs in the sky. Sometimes the most powerful miracle is sitting with yourself without flinching. That's what began to happen. No more mirrors as weapons. No more edits for God. Just a simple, sacred recognition: "I am who He says I am."

THE GOD WHO DELIGHTS

"The Lord your God is with you, the Mighty Warrior
who saves. He will take great delight in you; in his
love he will no longer rebuke you, but will rejoice
over you with singing." —Zephaniah 3:17

This verse captures something revolutionary about the divine nature, that God doesn't merely tolerate us or grudgingly accept us despite our flaws. God takes great delight in us, rejoices over us with singing, finds genuine joy in our existence.

The Hebrew word "sus" (delight) suggests not dutiful care but genuine affection, the kind of joy parents feel watching their children play, the delight lovers take in each other's presence. We are not burdens to be born or problems to be solved, but sources of divine pleasure and satisfaction.

The image of God singing over us with delight transforms our understanding of the divine relationship. This is not the stern judge waiting to pronounce sentence, not the disappointed parent cataloging our failures, but the God who finds such joy in our existence that He breaks into song.

PEACE BEYOND CIRCUMSTANCES

This truth didn't erase the pain I had experienced or magically restore what had been lost in my journey toward authenticity. The relationships that ended didn't suddenly resurrect themselves; the rejection didn't transform into acceptance. But it gave me something deeper and more lasting: peace.

Not the fragile peace that depends on having everything go right, not the conditional peace that requires others' approval, but the unshakeable peace that flows from knowing I belong, not just in this world, but in the very heart of God.

This peace doesn't fluctuate with my circumstances or depend on my performance. It doesn't increase when I do well or decrease when I struggle. It simply is as constant and reliable as the love from which it flows.

When I pray now, it's not with the trembling of a defendant before a harsh judge. It's with the trust of a beloved child speaking to a loving parent who delights in every word, who listens with complete attention, who responds with unfailing love. Prayer has transformed from a desperate attempt to convince God to love me into a natural conversation with the One who already does.

THE INVITATION HOME

"I have loved you with an everlasting love; I have drawn you with unfailing kindness." —Jeremiah 31:3

This promise reaches across time and circumstances to speak directly to every heart that has ever wondered if it is truly lovable. The love described here isn't temporary or conditional, it's everlasting, stretching from before our first breath to beyond our last.

There comes a moment, subtle and sacred, when you stop fighting yourself. When the masks fall, the noise hushes, and all that's left is the whisper that's been calling your name since the beginning. This moment wasn't a crescendo of thunder or the blaze of a miracle. It was silence, transparent and weightless.

I sat still. Not to perform. Not to plead. Just to be. And in that stillness, something ancient stirred inside me, not memory, but recognition.

"I love you. I have always loved you. I will always love you. Welcome home."

It didn't come as a shout or a chant or a sermon. It arrived like water meeting a thirsty root. Familiar, not because it had been said before, but because, in truth, it had always been true.

A WORD TO YOU

Now, I want to talk to you, not as a preacher or a teacher, but as a fellow traveler.

If you've ever wondered whether you are lovable, if you've lain awake at night questioning whether anyone could truly know you and still find you worthy of affection, let me tell you what I've learned through my own journey from performance to authenticity, from fear to faith:

You are lovable. Not potentially, not conditionally, not theoretically, but completely, and eternally lovable.

If you've ever wondered whether you are worthy, if you've measured yourself against impossible standards and found yourself lacking, the answer is yes, you are worthy. Not because you've earned it, not because you've proven it, but because worth is woven into the very fabric of your being.

If you've ever wondered whether you are enough, if you've felt the constant pressure to be more, do more, achieve more to justify your place in the world, hear this: You are enough. You have always been enough. You will always be enough.

You were created in the image of love itself, and absolutely nothing can change that foundational truth. Not your mistakes, not your struggles, not your questions or doubts. Not the opinions of others or the rejection of institutions. Not your past, not your present circumstances, not your uncertain future.

This truth isn't dependent on your understanding it, accepting it, or living up to it. It simply is. Like gravity or the rising of the sun, it operates independently of our belief in it.

LET YOURSELF BE FOUND

So, if your heart is searching, if you've been wandering through the wilderness of others' expectations, trying to find your way back to a sense of belonging, consider this: God is not far. Not distant in disapproval, not hidden behind barriers of performance or perfection, not waiting for you to somehow become more acceptable before drawing near.

God is not waiting for perfection because perfection was never the requirement. God is waiting for honesty, the simple, terrifying, liberating honesty of showing up as yourself, without editing or enhancement or apology.

Therefore, let yourself be seen. Not the carefully curated version you've been presenting, but the real, unedited, beautifully complex person you actually are. Let yourself be seen in your strength and your vulnerability, your certainty and your questions, your light and your shadow.

Let yourself be loved, not for who you pretend to be, but for who you actually are. Not despite your flaws and struggles, but as someone whose flaws and struggles are part of the beautiful, messy, sacred story of being human.

Let yourself be found, not by working harder to locate God in distant places or complicated systems, but by recognizing the divine presence that has never been absent from your life.

The mystic tradition speaks of this as "practicing the presence of God", not as a technique for accessing divine favor but as an awakening to what has always been true. The sacred is not confined to formal prayer or religious activities but is available in every moment, every task, every breath.

THE DOOR WAS NEVER CLOSED

There is strength in His love, not the brittle strength of performance or the fragile strength of earned approval, but the unshakeable strength of unconditional acceptance. There is peace in His presence, not the temporary peace of favorable circumstances, but the deep peace of knowing you belong exactly where you are. There is freedom in being exactly who He created you to be not the freedom of license, but the profound liberation of no longer having to be anyone other than yourself.

Come home to that truth. Stop wandering in the wilderness of others' opinions and expectations. Stop trying to find your worth in achievements or approval or the careful management of your image. Come home to the foundational reality of who you are and whose you are.

The image is clear: A house with warm light in the window, a table with your name already carved into the seat, a door never shut. Home is not where you arrive. Home is where you awaken.

Be you… fully, authentically, without apology or explanation. Be the complex, contradictory, beautiful person you were created to be. Be the one who carries questions alongside faith, who struggles and celebrates in equal measure, who reflects the divine image not through perfection but through authentic humanity.

And come home to the God who looks at you, really looks at you, seeing everything you've tried to hide and everything you've been afraid to reveal and says simply, with all the love that created the universe and holds it together:

"I love you. I have always loved you. I will always love you. Welcome home."

This is not theology. This is not doctrine. This is not religious theory. This is the lived reality available to every person who has ever felt lost or unworthy or afraid. This is the truth that transforms not just how we see ourselves, but how we move through the world as beloved children of a God who delights in our existence and sings over us with joy.

Come home. The door is open. The table is set. Love is waiting.

As Brené Brown once said: "Owning our story and loving ourselves through that process is the bravest thing we'll ever do."

I own this story now not the filtered version or the performance script, but the raw, radiant, sacred truth of it: the failures, the learning, the unbecoming, the becoming. And in doing so, I will make space for you to own yours, too.

If you remember nothing else, remember this:

You were never outside of love. You were never disqualified. You were never too far gone. Welcome home.

EPILOGUE

THE SOUND OF MY OWN VOICE

What I Know Now

Several years later, I wake up in a life that fits. It's smaller than the life I used to have, fewer people, simpler routines, less external validation. But it's mine in a way my previous life never was.

I know now that authenticity isn't a destination, it's a practice. Every day, I must choose honesty over comfort, truth over safety, growth over stagnation. Some days I fail. But the failures don't erase progress.

I know that love isn't always enough to bridge every distance, but it's always worth offering anyway. The relationships I lost taught me the value of the ones that remained. The family that rejected me helped me understand the chosen family that embraced me.

I know that courage isn't the absence of fear, it's the decision to act despite the fear. And that authenticity isn't about being perfect, it's about being real.

What I Hope You Know

If you're reading this while hiding some essential part of yourself, please know you are not broken. The world that tells you to be smaller, quieter, more palatable that world is broken. You are exactly as you were meant to be.

The cost of living your truth may be higher than you want to pay. It was higher than I wanted to pay. But the cost of not living it, the slow erosion of self, the weight of constant performance, the exhaustion of being a stranger in your own life that cost is higher still.

You don't owe anyone the version of you that makes them comfortable. You don't owe anyone your silence, your smallness, your suffering in service of their peace of mind.

You deserve to be known. Completely, fully, without reservation. You deserve love that doesn't require translation. You deserve a life that fits your actual shape, not the shape others have decided you should be.

The Sound of Freedom

There's a particular quality to laughter when it's unguarded, when it comes from a place that hasn't been edited or approved by committee. I hear that laughter in my own voice now sometimes, and it still surprises me.

This is what freedom sounds like: unscripted joy, uncalculated tears, words that come from the center of who you are rather than the edges of who you think you should be.

This is what healing looks like: not the absence of scars, but the presence of choice. The ability to write your own story, even if especially if it looks nothing like the story others wrote for you.

I am not the same man who stood in that third-grade classroom, learning to make himself smaller. I am not the man who spent decades in various closets, practicing how to disappear. I am not even the man who first said "I'm gay" in a Dallas bar, afraid of his own reflection.

I am who I have always been, finally brave enough to exist without apology.

And you, whoever you are, whatever truth you're carrying, whatever courage you're building you are exactly who you have always been too.

The only question left is: when will you be brave enough to let the world see?

"They called it confusion. But it was just me, learning to name every color of my soul."

ABOUT THE AUTHOR

Tedd Simmons has spent his adult life helping others discover and embrace who they were created to be, a calling that took on profound new meaning when he finally extended that grace to himself.

For thirteen years, he served as a minister, guiding congregations through questions of faith and identity. He then transitioned to corporate leadership as an HR executive, navigating the complex terrain of organizational culture and human potential. He has spent fifteen years in dual roles as both an HR executive and a business and life coach, supporting individuals and leaders in their journeys toward authentic living and professional excellence.

Tedd holds a Bachelor's degree from Anderson University, a Master of Arts and Master of Divinity from Anderson School of Theology, and a PhD in Organizational Leadership from Regent University. His diverse background in ministry, business, and coaching informs his understanding of the universal human struggle to reconcile who we are with who we're expected to be.

Currently, he lives in Florida with his husband and their dog, Cindy Crawford, where he continues his work as an HR executive, coach, and advocate for authenticity in all areas of life. Breathing Room is his first book.

URGENT PLEA!

Thank You For Reading My Book!

I really appreciate all of your feedback and
I love hearing what you have to say.

Please take two minutes now to leave a helpful review on
Amazon letting me know what you thought of the book

Thanks so much!

Tedd Simmons